Be Happy!

A 40 day journey to contentment

Peter Graystone

By the author of
Detox Your Spiritual Life in 40 Days

CANTERBURY
PRESS
Norwich

© Peter Graystone 2009

First published in 2009 by the Canterbury Press Norwich
Editorial office
13–17 Long Lane,
London, EC1A 9PN, UK

Canterbury Press is an imprint of Hymns Ancient and Modern Ltd
(a registered charity)
St Mary's Works, St Mary's Plain,
Norwich, NR3 3BH, UK

www.scm-canterburypress.co.uk

Scripture quotations taken from the Holy Bible, New International
Version. Copyright © 1973, 1978, 1984 by the International Bible
Society. Used by permission of Hodder & Stoughton Ltd, a member
of Hodder Headline Ltd.

British Library Cataloguing in Publication data

A catalogue record for this book is available
from the British Library

978-1-85311-972-9

Typeset by Regent Typesetting, London
Printed and bound in Great Britain by
CPI Bookmarque Croydon CR0 4TD

For Sarah

Be Happy!
Contents

Be Happy!
Introduction

When Charles de Gaulle, newly elected president of France, flew into England for a state visit in 1960, he brought his wife Yvonne. The politics of the day made the visit tense. The president was disgruntled that the Duchess of Kent was the only member of the royal family fluent enough in French to meet them at the airport. The attendant journalists did not help, but Madame de Gaulle was eager to please.

When they asked her, 'What are your hopes for the people of Britain?' the president's wife did her best with her limited English. She replied, 'I vont for every person in zis country to ave a penis.' As the journalists stepped back with a gasp, Charles de Gaulle leaned forward and explained to his wife, 'My dear, in England zey pronounce it *happiness*.'

I have started the book with this story because I want, for every person in this country, precisely what Yvonne de Gaulle wanted. (Let me clarify that! I want the thing she meant; not the thing she said!) And because of that, I have not only put my faith in following Jesus Christ, I have put my energy into sharing his Good News with as many people as I can. It is my belief that going through life accompanied by the living God can make you glad to be alive. Man, woman, child . . . you!

Not so long ago I asked someone from my church, 'Are you happy?'

She replied, 'No. But as a Christian you're not meant to be happy, are you? Instead, I try my hardest to be joyful.'

'What's the difference?' I asked.

As she floundered around and failed to think of an answer, I sensed her becoming tearful. And then I realized something important. When it comes to practical issues concerning the quality of your life, there is no real difference. A lack of happiness and a lack of joy are just as miserable as each other in a Christian life. But sometimes Christians feel confused or guilty that they do not have the happiness they believe God should be bringing them, and so they invent 'joy' as an alternative, gritting their teeth as they declare how hard they strive to achieve it.

That won't do!

I want you to be happy. I want the company of Jesus to make you glad to be alive.

That is why I am pleased that you are coming with me on this forty-day journey to seek happiness. Each chapter contains some thoughts about how changes in your attitudes and habits could make a significant difference to how happy you are. I don't promise that it will be easy, because it will affect every part of you – physical, emotional and spiritual. But I do promise that there will be plenty to enjoy along the way. All the stories are true, although occasionally I have changed people's names because I don't want to embarrass them. We will be accompanied on the route by the writers of the Bible and by inspiring Christians from history, who will be sharing their wisdom with us. And there will be practical suggestions and prayers as well.

One of my suggestions is that you talk about happiness with everyone you know. Ask people, 'What makes you happy?' Make it the most cheerful and talked-about subject for the next forty days. Write about it on your blog and on Facebook and Twitter. And if you want to tell me what you are discovering, contact me at be.happy.40.days@googlemail.com and I will do my best to reply.

My first prayer is that in forty days' time you will be a happier person. If you are, it won't be because this is a great book; it will be because we have a great God.

A happy mind

Be Happy!

Day I

Be content

Over the last couple of years I have been watching the salvation of someone. And a wonderful thing it has been! It hasn't happened in a rush. For someone with no Christian background at all to come to faith takes a long time, because it involves painstakingly turning every part of a life around. The *Ark Royal* doesn't spin on a saucer.

> There was a man all alone; he had neither son nor brother. There was no end to his toil, yet his eyes were not content with his wealth. 'For whom am I toiling,' he asked, 'and why am I depriving myself of enjoyment?' This too is meaningless – a miserable business!
>
> *Ecclesiastes 4.8*

So while I've been watching my friend become the person God has always planned him to be, I have had time to think about what it means to be saved by Jesus. I am embarrassed to confess that I used to talk about being saved without ever really thinking about what it is that Jesus actually saves us from. The Bible describes it in several ways – saved from oppression, from meaninglessness, from death, from sin. But the more I have thought about it, the more I have come to the conclusion that what this generation most needs to be saved from is discontent.

3

I don't mean greed. We all know that the love of money is the root of all evil. It is one of those verses from the New Testament that is so well known that even people who don't realize it comes from the Bible quote it. Rather, I mean discontent – the feeling that somehow the hand we have been dealt is not good enough. That restlessness for something better than what we've got – which is fine until it gets to the stage at which you can't enjoy what you *have* got because of it. And sadly I see that in churches almost as much as I see it in shopping malls.

The state of feeling ill at ease, and hankering after more, cannot possibly be how God intends his children to live. I've come to the conclusion that the most significant thing that God can do for this itchy, acquisitive generation is to make them glad to be alive. That is why I believe with all my heart in the salvation that Jesus can bring.

I'm not talking about being glad that we will be alive one day in heaven. I don't tell my friends that the point of being saved is to get to heaven and say to yourself, 'Ooh, I'm glad I'm dead!' The transforming thing about the Good News is that, no matter what your circumstances are – in your finances, relationships, achievements – Jesus can bring you to a point at which you say, 'Goodness, I'm glad to be alive!' As St Paul put it twenty centuries ago, 'As long as we have food and clothing, we can be content with that.'

> Godliness with contentment is great gain. For we brought nothing into the world, and we can take nothing out of it. But if we have food and clothing, we will be content with that. Those who want to get rich fall into temptation and a trap and into many foolish and harmful desires that plunge people into ruin and destruction. For the love of money is a root of all kinds of evil.
>
> I Timothy 6.6–10

Victorian preachers insisted that the secret of content was to accept the place that God had put you in the pecking order of society, and not fight against it. If you were poor, the best response was to get on with being poor without grumbling, and be as happy as you could. One of their favourite hymns included the words: 'The rich man in his castle, the poor man at the gate, God made them high and lowly, and ordered their estate.' Although children still sing 'All things bright and beautiful', no one sings that verse any more.

And of course, we don't think like that about God any more. We have learnt a lot about God during the last 200 years. One of the things we have learnt is that God doesn't want us to be content to leave some people in poverty while others get rich. The very opposite in fact! We should absolutely not be content to live in a comfortable country if that has come about at the cost of others being trapped in poverty. And surely God does not intend us to be apathetic, or content to let life drift by without attempting to improve ourselves.

So how do we know when to be content and when to agitate for something better?

Well ... my friend Gary came round for coffee and we were talking about my plumbing. Over Christmas my kitchen sink had been draining unbearably slowly. I told Gary that I would probably put up with it for a week, and when I couldn't stand it any longer I would pay for a plumber because I'm hopeless at DIY. Gary was adamant. 'Don't you dare! I'll stand over you and make you sort it out yourself.'

> True contentment is a real, active virtue. It is the power of getting out of any situation all there is in it.
>
> G. K. Chesterton, novelist, 1874–1936

And I did. Unscrewed all the wet, murky stuff! Cleared it! Saved a fortune! Felt triumphant!

It has really inspired me not to be content with my incompetence. Since then I've done a heap of work to improve my new flat – you should see the bathroom! So Gary and I have been discussing when it is right to be content, and when discontent should spur us on to make the world better. And it occurred to us that St Paul has already given us the answer. He wrote: 'Godliness with contentment is great gain.' That's how you know! Does the content you are hankering after in life come alongside godliness?

You can practise that! Practise being content with a godly approach to life. Practise lying in bed at the end of the day reflecting on any good things that have happened, and register that they are part of the world that God has spread out before us. Practise looking at your lunch before you eat it, with all its colours and smells and tastes, and thank God that he conceived such a sensual world for us. Practise focusing on what you enjoy about people, thanking God

> **The world is not enough.**
>
> *The family motto of Ian Fleming's hero James Bond, translated from the Latin 'Orbis non sufficit', which was the motto of the real life eighteenth-century financier Sir Thomas Bond*

that friendship and pleasure are possible in his good world. If you do that, God *will* make you a happier person.

> Lord God, I have been so eager to do well. But now turn me into someone who is eager to do good.
> Amen.

If you don't find content in godliness, there are plenty of people who will try to sell content to you. Many will persuasively tell you that you can find content in shiny, bleeping things. It starts with very young children who are offered content in hand-held, computerized, shiny, bleeping things. It escalates when adults are lured towards four-seater, shiny, bleeping things.

Or four-ring-hob, shiny, bleeping things. But now as then, godliness with contentment is great gain.

I'm writing to persuade myself as much as anyone else. Last week I got new curtains in the living room. (I was given some money to write this book!) And those curtains are making me unbelievably happy. But do you know what the source of that happiness is? It's not because they are new and shiny. It's because I put that curtain pole up myself. Drilled it, screwed it . . . and it's still up there! I keep going into the room to look at it and thank God. I am so content!

That's what this book is going to be about for the next forty days. About me, my home, my friends, and our hope that living our lives in the company of the risen Jesus will give us authentic happiness.

I must confess that I have been asking myself, 'Are people really going to be interested in my plumbing and my curtains?' But actually, those are the realities of life to which Jesus can genuinely make a difference. Don't be content just to let him change the way you pray on Sunday; expect him to change the way you live from Monday to Saturday. If you are going to turn the *Ark Royal*

> ### Be happy!
> Next time you have food in front of you, make a point of *not* saying grace – not in words anyway! Instead, look at what you are about to eat and drink, with its contrasting colours and textures, and anticipate the tastes that are on their way. Think about whether you are grateful for this. If you are, who are you grateful to?

round, then the curtains and the plumbing will be turning round with the rest of the ship.

Shiny, bleeping things – or godliness with contentment. Your choice!

Be Happy!

Day 2

Let go of grievances

When I got my first job as a teacher in a primary school, I moved out of my parents' home and bought a flat in South London. I chose one on a council estate where the children I was teaching lived, because I thought that had more integrity. To those who came and visited me there, thank you for the happy memories – and I'm sorry about your wing mirrors!

It had stretched me as far as I could to buy the place, so I thought I was quite poor. But I was naive, and I got a shock when I found myself living among people who really were poor. I got on very well with Suzanne, whose front door was opposite mine. I admired her terrifically because she was putting grim family circumstances behind her and bringing up her little boy Joel to rise above them. It was the first time it had occurred to me that some people live in a house with no carpet, so I was learning a great deal in a short time.

> [Jesus said,] 'Blessed are the peacemakers, for they will be called children of God.'
>
> *Matthew 5.9*

One of Suzanne's relatives died in Leeds, and she got the chance to go and take any furniture she wanted. For her, it was like stumbling on hidden treasure, and she asked if I could help. I hired a lorry, put the couple of hundred pounds it cost on my credit card, and we drove up there. We loaded the furniture, brought it home, and it transformed the flat. Fantastic! The deal was that she would give me £5 a month until she had paid me back, which I could cope with as long as I was careful not to buy anything frivolous. When the next month came round, she couldn't manage to make the first payment, so I said she should wait for another month before she started paying. But the next month a crisis arose, and she put it off again. It was the same the following month, and I began to realize that I was never going to see any of the money again. This was, to be honest, a bit of a problem for me financially.

> Bear with each other and forgive whatever grievances you may have against one another. Forgive as the Lord forgave you. And over all these virtues put on love, which binds them all together in perfect unity. Let the peace of Christ rule in your hearts.
>
> *Colossians 3.13–15*

But the worst thing was that each time I met Suzanne, virtually every other day, one or other of us was having to bring up the subject of the money. I felt really bad about it, and she must have felt worse. Soon I found myself checking through the spy glass in the front door before I went out because I didn't want to meet her accidentally and have to acknowledge this grievance between us. And

> Pardon one another so that later on you will not remember the injury. The remembering of an injury is itself a wrong: it adds to our anger, feeds our sin and hates what is good. It is a rusty arrow and poison for the soul.
>
> *Francis of Paola, founder of an Italian monastic order, 1416–1507*

one day, out of the corner of my eye, I spotted that she was doing exactly the same, and I realized that the relationship had been ruined.

This was miserable, because all the joy of the fact that she now had a sofa and a wardrobe had turned into a burden because of the debt. I had a long think about it, and finally decided that the only thing I could do was to let go of the money, pretend it had never happened, and get the friendship back on track. So I went and told her that a wealthy person at my church had offered to pay off my credit card. This was a complete lie, so the ninth commandment will probably be nailed to my coffin! In fact, I had to make a few sacrifices to get out of the mess, but it completely solved the problem between us.

However, there was something I hadn't expected, and that was the tidal wave of relief that flooded over me once I had let go of this grievance that had come between us. I felt renewed and happy. In fact, even remembering it today has brought back some of that joy of a burden lifting.

> Everyone says forgiveness is a lovely idea until they have something to forgive.
>
> C. S. Lewis, writer and academic, 1898–1963

After that I kept looking at other people on the estate and noticing those who had lost their happiness over conflicts and sores which they just couldn't let go. A man who was exhausting himself into misery in a dispute with the council, from whom he was trying to get compensation because he broke his ankle by tripping in the street. Another man who hadn't spoken to his brother for a decade over a refusal to apologize and had sunk into a depression that was disabling every aspect of his life. A woman who sat virtually all day by her back window with a glass of water to throw at her neighbour's cat if it set foot in her garden – a source of constant bickering between them. And I kept thinking, 'Why don't you just let go of this stuff? Just let go of it! You don't have to be religious about it. You don't have to worry that you haven't had the last word, or got what you deserved.

You don't even have to tell anyone what you've done. Just let go! Make up your mind that these grievances are not going to have any power over you from now on. And feel the life-giving freedom of being a peacemaker.'

> God of peace, release me from the need to have the last word, the best deal, the winning argument. Instead give me back the freedom of friendship. And then let me call you father.
> Amen.

Blessed are the peacemakers. Or in the nearest English equivalent to Jesus' original saying: 'Congratulations to you peacemakers!'

Congratulations to you who summon the patience to stop snapping at someone and start listening to them instead. Congratulations to you who talk long into the night with people who feel lost, and lead them gently to the peace of forgiveness. Congratulations to you who succeed in letting go of a grievance and restoring a relationship. Does it mean you have released someone from a burden? No! It's the other way round. By forgiving someone you release the hold they have on you – that is why Jesus said you will be blessed if you succeed in making peace.

And your reward? God knows you as his son or his daughter. Why is that? Because when he sees what you have done, he recognizes a faint, flickering image of his own dear child, Jesus.

So give it a try! Let go! Just let go of the things that have disrupted the peace between you and someone else, and see what happens. You've got nothing to lose. After all, if it doesn't work, there's nothing to stop you going back to the hate and tension again. You won't be any worse off! But maybe . . . who knows?

There's no guarantee it will be easy to be called a child of God. If you doubt that, just remember what happened to the original Child of God in the years that followed him talking about making peace during a sermon he gave on a hill overlooking Lake Galilee.

Be happy!

Bring to mind the people or organizations who have slighted you, or hurt your feelings. People or businesses who owe you something, material or intangible, or with whom you need to get even. Think about the ways in which these things have held you back. Weigh up for a while whether it would be possible for you to write off these debts as if they had never happened. Make up your mind to try living as if they have no power over you at all, perhaps just for a trial period. There is no need to tell anyone that you have forgiven them. But monitor whether you have more peace of mind now that you have let go of the weight you were dragging around.

But give it a go! Blessed are the peacemakers. Children of God. Just let go of stuff. Be glad! Congratulations!

Be Happy!

Day 3

Master your worries

Why Jesus? Because he was utterly practical about how to live a worthwhile life. He calmed anxiety. His advice worked.

He spoke to the widow – lonely and debilitated out of fear for the future. He spoke to the man sinking under debt – worrying where the strength would come from to get a foothold. He spoke to those who were so anxious about material things that there was no room to grow in peace, joy and love – those who had reached that terrible state because they were so poor, and those who were in the same trap because they were so rich.

> What do people get for all the toil and anxious striving with which they labour under the sun? All their days their work is pain and grief; even at night their minds do not rest. This too is meaningless. People can do nothing better than to eat and drink and find satisfaction in their work.
>
> *Ecclesiastes 2.22–24*

So when Jesus says, 'Don't worry!' you know he isn't just patting people on the head and saying, 'There, there!' Rather, he is intent on improving people's lives. And I'm the kind of person who needs to be persuaded that there is a reason not to be anxious. I'm a born worrier.

After I left school, aged eighteen, I worked in a warehouse while I was waiting for my exam results to come out. I worried endlessly about whether I'd studied hard enough to get into college. I remember the forklift truck driver saying to me: 'What's the point of getting anxious about college? You can't quote Shakespeare when you're dead.

My religion is: There's no worry on earth that can't be put right by a cold lager and a hot woman.'

Well, I've had several cold lagers since then!

I think about what he said from time to time, because more or less his exact words appear in the Bible. The man who wrote the book of Ecclesiastes was every bit as cynical as the driver. Jesus must have known these words: 'What do people get for all the toil and anxious striving with which they labour under the sun? People can do nothing better than to eat and drink and find satisfaction in their work.'

It seems impossible that these sarcastic words are in the Bible!

> [Jesus said,] 'Who of you by worrying can add a single hour to your life? Since you cannot do this very little thing, why do you worry about the rest? Consider how the lilies grow. They do not labour or spin. Yet I tell you, not even Solomon in all his splendour was dressed like one of these. If that is how God clothes the grass of the field, which is here today, and tomorrow is thrown into the fire, how much more will he clothe you, O you of little faith! And do not set your heart on what you will eat or drink; do not worry about it. For the pagan world runs after all such things, and your Father knows that you need them. But seek his kingdom, and these things will be given to you as well.
>
> *Luke 12.25–31*

But of course, just because they are in the Bible, it doesn't mean the Bible approves of them. Ecclesiastes is one of the parts of the Bible that tells you, 'This is how people in your world will think, but it's *not* how the people of God are to think.' Rise above this! Rise above it. Find a better way.

And of course, Jesus did find a better way. This was his contrasting advice: 'Do not worry about your life, what you will eat; or about your body, what you will wear. Life is more than food, and the body more than clothes.' It is as if Jesus deliberately set out to give the writer of Ecclesiastes a slap in the face: 'How dare you be so cynical!' And I'll bet he would say the same to the warehouse guy as well.

> Pardon me and pray for me. Pray for me, I say. For I am sometimes so fearful, that I would creep into a mouse-hole. Sometimes God doth visit me again with his comfort. So he cometh and goeth.
>
> *Hugh Latimer, Bishop of Worcester, in a letter from prison to his friend Bishop Nicholas Ridley, shortly before he was put to death for his faith, 1485–1555*

Anxiety is going to be a fact of life, but there are two ways of responding to it. One of them is: 'Blot it out with whatever you can find – in a bottle, in a fridge, in a shopping mall, or by working so hard that you never have to deal with it.' That's the cynic's way.

Alternatively, there is the way of Jesus, who says, 'My method won't blot out worry. Or magic it away. But I can give you a secure way of dealing with it. Do you want to know more?'

Of course we want to know more! Jesus gives us three

> I worry until midnight, and from then on I let God worry.
>
> *Luigi Guanella, founder of an Italian monastic order, 1842–1915*

straightforward reasons why we shouldn't worry. The first one that it's pointless. Jesus, though, said it rather more poetically: 'Who of you by worrying can add a single hour to his life? Since you cannot do this very little thing, why do you worry about the rest?'

The average English woman lives 709,560 hours. If you spend all the waking ones worrying that this is not enough, will you live one more? Not a chance! So do something more practical than worrying. If you are lying in bed unable to sleep, form a plan for the next day. When you've made up your mind what you are going to do, tell yourself that you have done everything you can and that you will just have to hand over to God the things that are out of your control. There is no guarantee that this will get you to sleep, but it makes far better use of the boring, wakeful hours than letting anxiety spin out of control.

The second reason is that worrying shows a lack of faith in God's ability to provide. Once again, Jesus' version is wonderfully memorable: 'If God clothes the grass of the field, which is here today, and tomorrow is thrown into the fire, how much more will he clothe you.'

God of every living thing, I don't ask you to blot out everything that makes me anxious. But I do ask for reassurance that you are very close to me in this worrisome world.
Amen.

Tell yourself, when you are full of anxiety, that this is what you are a Christian for. Moments like these! This is the time when people who have no faith have nothing to turn to. But in contrast, it is the time when all those minutes you have spent in prayer with God, added up over 709,560 hours, will strengthen you in a unique way. So assert at moments of high anxiety: 'I may be worried, but in God I have something precious – and now is the time to call on it to sustain me.'

And the third reason: if you are a Christian, there is no need to be preoccupied with the same things that the rest of the world frets over: 'Do not set your heart on what you will eat or drink; do not worry about it. For the pagan world runs after all such things.'

I remember the first time that the very different way Christians can think came home to me. While I worked in that warehouse all my friends were passing their driving tests and practising their negotiating skills by getting their parents to lend them a car on a Saturday night. I recall one of my friends coming out of my home and finding that, while his mother's car was parked, someone had dented the wing. So there was *great* deal of worrying that evening, and I went with him in case breaking the news turned out to be traumatic. But his mother's first words were: 'It's a thing, not a person. First of all tell me whether you are OK.' And I can remember thinking, 'Good grief! That's how Christians prioritize matters. That's not what I expected at all.'

> ### Be happy!
> Think back ten years. What age were you? What were the things that were worrying you most then? And what were you most worried about five years ago? And twelve months ago? What are your feelings today about the anxieties you had then? Now make a list of the things that worry you most now. Be frank with God about how you feel about them, and then wait to see whether God will be equally frank with you.

It still stays with me, that happy memory. It's one of the many, many reasons I now follow Jesus. The logic of his reassurance still speaks to me across 2,000 years (that's 17,520,000 hours). God's care for all I can see – flowers, birds, fields – gives me confidence for all I *can't* see. He is at work in that as well. So master your worries!

Be Happy!

Day 4

Get real about love

It's just after Easter in Tenerife. I'm on holiday with my gorgeous godchildren and their family. Mum and Dad have gone to a meeting because some chav in a Primark suit is trying to sell them a timeshare. So I've had seven-year-old Anna and five-year-old William since breakfast. We've done the mini golf, we've done the swimming pool, and now we're going for a walk along the beach. And a charming little voice floats up: 'I do love you, Peter.'

> If I speak in human or angelic tongues, but have not love, I am only a resounding gong or a clanging cymbal. If I have the gift of prophecy and can fathom all mysteries and all knowledge, and if I have a faith that can move mountains, but have not love, I am nothing. If I give all I possess to the poor and surrender my body to the flames, but have not love, I gain nothing.
>
> *1 Corinthians 13.1–3*

I reply, 'Oh what a lovely thing to say! I love you too. Both of you!'

There is a brief silence, and then I hear, 'Have you noticed that the beach shop is selling chocolate ice creams?'

The little rascal – I nearly fell for it!

It gave me a problem, because Anna and William have a

strict holiday rule about having only one ice cream per day. Anna is the biggest girl in her class, but William is a minute scrap for his age. When they are playing on the beach they look a comical pair. William doesn't look like her brother; he looks like her lunch. So you can understand why Mum and Dad want to make sure they eat well and wisely. It makes me miserable to say no to such terrific children. But I think it is genuinely more loving to stick to the rule than to sneak in an extra Cornetto.

Sometimes we say I love you, and it has nothing to do with authentic love. Sometimes we say, 'You can't have what you want,' and we do it *because* we love the person. Love is so complicated. We have got used to love having a price-tag attached to it. We expect something back.

> Love is patient, love is kind. It does not envy, it does not boast, it is not proud. It is not rude, it is not self-seeking, it is not easily angered, it keeps no record of wrongs. Love does not delight in evil but rejoices with the truth. It always protects, always trusts, always hopes, always perseveres. Love never fails.
>
> *1 Corinthians 13.4–8*

'Love is complicated' does not appear in the long list of facts about love that Paul wrote in one of his letters, twenty years after the life of Jesus. But it should have done!

Just like you can mistake ice cream for love, people seeking happiness are wide open to mistaking other things for love. So Paul wrote to his friends in Corinth about how you tell love – the real thing – from the ice cream versions. This is actually the subject of most chick flick movies. Teenagers could save themselves six quid and ninety minutes with Kirsten Dunst, and instead use Paul's words as a checklist to find out what is going on with a girlfriend or boyfriend. Is what is happening in this relationship patient, or am I being pushed too far too fast? Is it self-seeking, or are both people preferring to seek each other's happiness? Is the other person using this relationship to boast to friends? Or am I?

Well, if love involves any of those things it is not going to lead to lasting happiness. Paul knew that – twenty centuries before we had *Sex and the City* to tell us. 'Love is patient, love is kind. It does not boast, it is not self-seeking.'

But Paul's words are a practical guide for worshippers as well. He is very scornful of people whose highlight is to go to a church service because they like a good sing. Or a good sermon, or any kind of emotional high! These things are not, according to Paul, what being a Christian is about.

> Christ has made love the stairway that would enable all Christians to climb up to heaven. So hold fast to love in all sincerity. Give each other practical proof of it. And by your progress in it, make the ascent together.
>
> *Fulgentius of Ruspe, bishop in North Africa, 468–533*

And nor (and this is rather unsettling) is faith the most significant thing about a Christian life. I suspect Paul may have been thinking of that hard-nosed, intolerant kind of Christian faith that despises any other point of view except a particular version of the truth. The kind of faith that allows someone to give every last penny to a charity for converting the poor of Africa, but cuts off a family member because he or she has made a moral decision that doesn't fit a particular version of the truth.

For all the good that kind of worship or that kind of faith does, you might as well stand in a corner and bang a gong. Or as he put it: 'If I speak in human tongues or sing in angelic tongues, but have not love, I am only a resounding gong or a clanging cymbal. If I have a faith that could move mountains, if I give all I possess to the poor, but have not love, I'm nothing.'

This is all a bit disconcerting. You hear the part of the Bible in which Paul wrote about love read at weddings.

> 'And did you get what you wanted from this life, even so?'
> I did.
> 'And what did you want?'
> To call myself beloved.
> To feel myself beloved on the earth.
>
> Raymond Carver, North American poet, 1938–88

But, to be honest, you're not really in the mood at a wedding to think troubling things about what it means to be a Christian. You just want the moment to be romantic and the best man not to drop the rings!

But the famous words are actually a plea to a Christian community to get its priorities right so that there can be genuine happiness among them. Be driven by love, not by ice cream – in your romantic relationships, in your worship of God, in your relationships with others in the church, in the way you treat everyone with whom you engage from tomorrow onwards.

Please, says Paul, don't have relationships with your parents ruined by resentments for things they did years ago that have shaped your life. Try to find a way through that with love, because 'love does not keep an endless record of wrongs'. Please don't have no-go areas in a church so as to avoid people with whom you have fallen out over the rota for flower-arranging. Try to find a way through that with love, because 'love is not easily angered'. Please

> Lord God, fill my whole being with love. Not the slushy kind or the greedy kind, but the kind that will help people I know be sure that their lives are worth living.
> Amen.

don't find yourself secretly pleased when a friend doesn't get the promotion that would have got them to a place one better than you. Try to find a way through that with love, because 'love does not envy, it does not delight in evil'. Please don't give up when your attempt to reach out to a fellow human being is met with a lack of gratitude. Try to find a way through that with love, because 'love always perseveres; it never fails'.

> ### Be happy!
> Make a mental list of those you love. (This is not the same as the list of those whom you feel you ought to love.) It will probably consist mainly of people, but there is no reason why you shouldn't include animals or even places and activities if it is easier to think of them than men and women. Read the list of qualities of love from the Bible that appears earlier in the chapter, and dwell on how it relates to those in your thoughts. For the situations where you recognize that the love you have is absolutely real, be happy. If you have ended up with some challenging questions, I am hoping that the chapters to come will help you work out what to do in response.

Risk getting real about love. It may lead to some things you assumed to be love melting like a choc ice. It may lead to you recognizing as love some things that you had thought were just unremitting hard work. Love almost certainly won't look like what you expect it to be. But the real thing, even at the cost of sacrifice and tears, will make you happy.

In front of me on the desk is a lilac envelope. Inside is a drawing of a man with an exceedingly round, bald head. There are hearts fluttering all around it like butterflies. The message says, in very wobbly handwriting, 'Please come on holiday with us again soon.' I believe I am loved.

Be Happy!
Day 5
Come clean

One of the joys of listening to a story is being one step ahead of the storyteller. We hear thousands of stories in a lifetime, and from our earliest days we become canny at recognizing what lies ahead. So when someone begins, 'I want to tell you a tale about Ivan the Terrible,' we already know that it's not going to be about how he won everyone's hearts through his skill at flower-arranging. Likewise, we don't settle down to listen to a legend about St Agnes the Chaste expecting to hear how she used her seductive

> To some who ... looked down on everybody else, Jesus told this parable: 'Two men went up to the temple to pray, one a Pharisee and the other a tax collector. The Pharisee stood up and prayed about himself: "God, I thank you that I am not like other men – robbers, evildoers, adulterers – or even like this tax collector. I fast twice a week and give a tenth of all I get." But the tax collector stood at a distance. He would not even look up to heaven, but beat his breast and said, "God, have mercy on me, a sinner." I tell you that this man, rather than the other, went home justified before God. For everyone who exalts himself will be humbled, and he who humbles himself will be exalted.'
>
> *Luke 18.9–14*

feminine wiles to lure innocents to a hideous slaughter. The name gives it away!

A good storyteller can catch us out. And Jesus was a very good storyteller! But sometimes we are so familiar with his stories that we forget how good he was. For instance, as soon as we encounter a Pharisee in the Bible, we know he is going to come out of the story badly. We automatically assume that a Pharisee was a bad influence on the world. But to Jesus' original hearers Pharisees represented something good about the world, and it was shocking that he criticized them. Pharisees did wonderful things for the culture and religion of the time. In the dust and heat of Jerusalem they went without water two days a week in order to pray for their nation. That puts me to shame!

There were about 6,000 Pharisees. They were a middle-class Jewish pressure group united by a passionate commitment to the holiness of God. They were convinced that the standards of their society were in decline, and believed that the dreadful things that had befallen Israel had come about because people had been disobedient to God's laws in their day-to-day behaviour. They gave themselves the task of expanding those rules to give specific instructions for how to live in every single area of a person's life. They were a good and necessary thing! But they knew it, and that was the problem!

> Who is a God like you, who pardons sin? ...
> You do not stay angry for ever but delight to show mercy.
> You will again have compassion on us; you will ... hurl all our iniquities into the depths of the sea.
>
> *Micah 7.18–19*

In contrast to the crowds who were listening to Jesus' captivating tales, a tax collector had an altogether different reputation. The Jews of Jesus' time were a race who had been overrun by a foreign superpower and were subject to military occupation. The Roman empire that ruled the Jews by might had conquered them because it needed the economic clout that these people, who lived on a profitable trade route, could bring. So the Roman authorities had

> Humanity is never so beautiful as when praying for forgiveness or else forgiving another.
>
> John Paul Richter, German novelist, 1763–1825

forcibly established a method of collecting taxes from their conquered people, who obviously loathed having to pay. They employed Jewish people to collect the taxes from their own countrymen. Clearly these people were going to be despised by their own, because effectively they were collaborating with the enemy. Why would anyone do that? Money! It was because the Romans allowed the tax collectors to set their own rate of commission on top of the revenue they were collecting. So they were the kind of people who would tolerate being despised in order to be rich. Wealthy traitors!

So who would you expect to come out well from a story about a Pharisee and a tax collector? It's like putting St Agnes up against Tsar Ivan.

Well, when Jesus told that story, the St Agnes figure emerged terribly. The Pharisee was standing in front of a God who is perfect and almighty, and trying to establish that somehow he was good enough to earn God's respect. He told God about

> If I can now forgive, it is only because I have been forgiven – I and all other men and women who have ever lived.
>
> John Austin Baker, English bishop, born 1928

the sins he had not committed. He stressed how he had faithfully kept all the correct religious rules. And he compared himself favourably to others.

Oh dear! You know, I've found myself doing all those things. I've read about people who have done terrible things while professing to be Christians and thought to myself, 'Well, at least I've never done anything that bad.' And I sometimes write a chapter of a book and think to myself, 'I come out of this rather well, don't I?' All that might make me impressive in other people's eyes, but it does nothing for me in God's eyes!

Why does the Ivan the Terrible character come out of the story well? Because the tax collector stooped before God precisely as he was. No pretence! He was completely honest with God about how he was, even though he felt grim, remorseful, unworthy.

The truth about us comes out when we are praying. Not when we are praying aloud for others to hear, but when we are alone with God. He will never turn a deaf ear to someone who is telling the truth about his or her feelings. 'God, I am angry that you have allowed this to happen.' God listens and God cares. 'God, this is a desperate situation and I need help.' God listens and God cares. 'God, I am bored, and praying is the last thing I feel like doing.' God listens and God cares. 'God, I'm not even sure you are there.' God listens and God cares.

> Lord God, the truth is that I am not the best person in the world, but I am not the worst either. I am just me. Despite everything I am, and because of everything you are, have mercy I pray.
> Amen.

And now I am going to tell you the most important thing I have discovered in all my years, so with all my heart I hope that you are in a quiet place when you read it.

God loves you. He loves you completely and entirely. He will never love you more than he does at this moment. Even if you become a Christian tomorrow he will not love you more than he does today. He can't, because he loves you perfectly already. His love is absolute and has no qualifications attached to it at all.

But this liberating fact does not stop there. The truth is that not only will God never love you more, he will also never love you less. If you don't pray to him this week he won't love you less. If you don't open a Bible this year he won't love you less. If you never go to church again he won't love you less. That is the freedom of worshipping a God who loves with no conditions, the God of grace.

That is why our God is one before whom you can be completely honest. You see, in heaven we will meet people like the tax collector – who felt he was worthless, but whose integrity shines out in Jesus' story. People like that are forgiven in the grace of God.

But in heaven we will also meet people like the Pharisee – who tried so hard, but whose love and humility were notably missing that day in the temple. People like that are also forgiven in the grace of God. That is the extent of how loving God is.

Anything you have done – a lifetime of churchgoing, the decades of goodness, the effort of trying to get things right – is unimportant right at this moment. All God needs is for you to come in humility, saying, 'Have mercy on me, Lord.' And he will draw you to his lovely presence, whether you deserve it or whether you don't. Amazing!

> **Be happy!**
> Sit for a few minutes, holding out empty hands. Just like the tax collector, tell God exactly how you are. Tell him your doubts and your hopes. Tell him the secrets you wouldn't tell me. Tell him you're sorry today, if that's true. Tell him you have nothing to be sorry about today, if that's true. Tell him what you want. He knows already, but he will deeply value the honesty.

Be Happy!

Day 6

Make yourself known

I don't have much experience of sheep. I've been a Croydon man all my life, and you have to go quite a way from South London in order to get close to one. On a shelf in my bedroom I have a toy lamb that I have had since the day I was born, now patched and bald, but I don't think that counts.

Having said that, it is my friend Paul's twenty-fifth birthday today, and if I can get this chapter written in the next three hours, I am hoping to get thoroughly acquainted

> Jesus said again, 'I tell you the truth, I am the gate for the sheep. All who ever came before me were thieves and robbers, but the sheep did not listen to them. I am the gate; whoever enters through me will be saved. He will come in and go out, and find pasture. The thief comes only to steal and kill and destroy; I have come that they may have life, and have it to the full ... I am the good shepherd; I know my sheep and my sheep know me – just as the Father knows me and I know the Father – and I lay down my life for the sheep. I have other sheep that are not of this sheep pen. I must bring them also. They too will listen to my voice, and there shall be one flock and one shepherd.'
>
> *John 10.7–16*

with a sheep at his barbecue this lunchtime. So I am going to say something that may be completely uninformed and insensitive, but everything I've glimpsed of rural life has led me to believe this: sheep are pig-ignorant. (I also think that pigs are sheep-ignorant, but that's a subject for a different book.)

You don't have to observe sheep for too long to work this out. Just watch them trying to decide which way to go when they have no one to guide them. They follow a leader from among them- selves in what appears to be an orderly way. The problem is that their leader doesn't know the way and is as likely to lead them to disaster as to security. That's the context in which Jesus described him- self as a good shepherd. He pictured his society as 'harassed and helpless, like sheep without a shepherd'. I often think of his description of that generation when I look at our own. How did we get to a state in which we take moral ad- vice from a runner-up on *Big Brother*, or emotional advice from an astrologer in a TV guide? If ever there was a time when we needed a good shepherd, it's now.

> Shout for joy to the Lord, all the earth.
> Worship the Lord with gladness;
> come before him with joyful songs.
> Know that the Lord is God.
> It is he who made us, and we are his;
> we are his people, the sheep of his pasture.
>
> Psalm 100.1–3

To get the hang of what Jesus meant you have to leave the lamb chops cooking on the barbecue and travel back 2,000 years. Pic- ture sheep grazing on a

> The king of love my shepherd is,
> Whose goodness faileth never;
> I nothing lack if I am his
> And he is mine for ever.
>
> Henry Baker, clergyman and hymn- writer, 1821–77

hillside in the days of Jesus – the image that his original audience would have had in their minds. In the valley is a sheep pen with rock walls in the shape of a horseshoe, with a narrow entrance. It is evening, so the sheep have been led into the pen. The shepherd is lying across the entrance. He is asleep – well, it's an exhausting job! But he has trained himself to wake at any moment should there be a disturbance. If a sheep nudges his body to try to escape, he's wide awake, shoving it back in. If a wild animal or, worse still, a thief attempts to climb across him to find a free supper, he is instantly alert and ready to protect his flock.

The shepherd is a real human gate. He is literally 'laying down his life for the sheep'. When Jesus says, 'I am the gate for the sheep,' that's what his audience imagines. What a marvellous picture! It's about security, but it's also about freedom. For those whom life has cramped and confined, like sheep cooped up in a pen, Jesus is claiming to be the exit to the liberty of the pastures – out of oppression into freedom. For those whom life has frightened and bruised, he is the entrance into the security of the fold – out of loneliness into protection.

As Jesus pointed out, there are plenty of people prepared to *sell* you these kinds of security and freedom. Hence the celebrities, the astrologers, and a forest of self-help books. But absolutely none have the integrity of Jesus. He called them 'hired hands' – not real shepherds at all. Hired hands run away when a wolf comes anywhere near. What Jesus meant was that a religious fraud offers us spiritual fulfilment for money and is absolutely useless when a crisis arises. But Jesus offers it for love and stays with us no matter what it costs him.

> Stay close to Jesus.
>
> *Paul the Great, Egyptian desert father (hermit), about 300–50*

It sounds fantastic and life-transforming. It *is* fantastic and life-transforming. 'I have come that they may have life, and have it to the full.' Fabulous! How do we respond? Well, sheep can be obstinate creatures. And let's be honest, so can we! But the astonishing thing is that a good shepherd does not love them even a tiny bit less because of that.

What does Jesus the good shepherd tell us about the relationship he has with his sheep? First, he identifies each of them individually. Now, when your closest encounter with a sheep is a kebab shop, that is astonishing. When I look at a flock of sheep, do I see twenty-three individual creatures whom I know by name and can identify by their particular bleat? No, I do not! I see a couple of dozen white woolly blobs. In contrast, Jesus claims that all six billion humans who are alive on this planet are individually known by him, as are the other six billion who have lived in history.

And second, he relates to each one of them intimately. And that too is an extraordinary discovery for people like me who only want sheep to be intimate once they come in sweater format. 'I know my sheep and my sheep know me,' Jesus says. 'Just as the Father knows me and I know the Father.' He knows each one of us as uniquely as he knows God. Amazing! Trust the shepherd.

> Lord Jesus, it's me. I realize that I'm not the only one talking to you right now. But I am the only one with this unique set of needs, anxieties and hopes. I am so grateful that you intimately understand every aspect of me. I know it doesn't instantly solve all the problems. But it's a mighty fine starting point. So thank you.
> Amen.

But such a relationship is never exclusive. Jesus' original Jewish hearers must have assumed that they alone were God's people. But Jesus speaks of 'other sheep' who would come from different religions to swell the church. And he was quite explicit about it: 'I have other sheep that are not of this sheep pen. I must bring them also.'

Jesus' words are a warning today to anyone who thinks they can draw boundaries to prescribe who is part of the good shepherd's flock and who isn't. Jesus is answerable to no one but God himself. Not even death can tell him what to do. Jesus will save whom he will save, and that will not be dictated by race, by morality, by religion, or by any lines we humans like to draw in order to make it seem that we are the special ones and someone else isn't. It will be dictated by love. Nothing else, just love! The love that was so extreme that it drove Jesus to lay down his life for the sake of humankind. When you see the unexpected millions who are beside you in the great multitude that meets Jesus in heaven, prepare to feel sheepish!

That is why having a good shepherd truly is a reason for happiness. Thrilling, isn't it! And it has thrilled people the world over, because there is something about the image of being looked after and guided that appeals universally. Wherever the Bible is translated, the image is developed to be appropriate to the local setting. In South America the sheep become llamas; in the Himalayas they are yaks; in parts of Africa they are goats.

And in Croydon? Well, in Croydon they're lunch. And I'm already ten minutes late. But when I drive over to Paul's I shall be bouncing with joy in the car. Oh yes indeed!

> **Be happy!**
> Look round your home for wool – in clothes, in carpet, in fabrics. Take a few strands in your fingers, and think about the many other hands through which they have passed on their way to you. All strangers to you; all known to and loved by God. He has every strand numbered. And every human named!

Be Happy!
Day 7
Push past pain

As a teenager in the fourteenth century a woman who lived in Norfolk, whose name is long forgotten, successfully pleaded with her bishop to be allowed the honour of becoming an anchorite. This means that she was bricked up in a room, next to St Julian's Church in Norwich, which she never left, in order to devote herself to a life of worship. There she lived, prayed and contemplated God until she was seventy. And wrote – she was the first woman to

> I remember my affliction and my wandering,
> the bitterness and the gall.
> I well remember them,
> and my soul is downcast within me.
> Yet this I call to mind
> and therefore I have hope:
> Because of the Lord's great love we are not consumed,
> for his compassions never fail.
> They are new every morning;
> great is your faithfulness.
> I say to myself, 'The Lord is my portion;
> therefore I will wait for him.'
>
> *Lamentations 3.19–24*

have a book published in the English language! Her cell is still there in Norwich, and visiting it is very moving.

Aged thirty, she had a life-threatening illness. In fact, she believed she was about to fall victim to the Black Death, which was devastating Europe. In intense pain, she had a series of visions of Jesus, during which profound truths about life became clear. When she recovered, she wrote them down in an unremittingly optimistic book called *Sixteen Revelations of Divine Love*. It is still in print today, under the name by which the world knows her – Julian of Norwich.

There is a slanted window in the wall of the cell, and through it you can squint into the church and fix your eyes (as she did) on the cross on the altar. Next to the window are written some of her words, composed at the height of her ill health: 'These words, "You will not be overcome," were said very insistently and strongly, for certainty and strength against every tribulation which may come. He did not say, "You will not be troubled, you will not be belaboured, you will not be disquieted," but he said, "you will not be overcome." God wants us to pay attention to these words and always to be strong in faithful trust, in well-being and in woe, for he loves and delights in us, and so he wishes us to love him and delight in him and trust greatly in him. And all shall be well. And all shall be well. And all manner of thing shall be well.'

> Consider it pure joy, my brothers and sisters, whenever you face trials of many kinds, because you know that the testing of your faith develops perseverance. Perseverance must finish its work so that you may be mature and complete, not lacking anything.
>
> James 1.2–4

In the heart of the Old Testament is a set of poems that agonize over the destruction of Jerusalem in 587 BC. In our Bible they have the name

Lamentations. The poems grieve over the suffering of loved ones and the devastation wreaked on the walls of a beloved city. But they are desolate about something worse – God seemed to have abandoned his people. But at his low point the poet's complete loss of hope acted as a trigger to bring him to his spiritual senses, as if despair left him nowhere else to go but to God. To recall that God is still sustaining life, and consciously to seek a reason to thank him daily, does not spring easily from the human heart. It is an act of will that only the grace of God can uphold.

Between agreeing to write this book and starting the first chapter, I had a shock that made me question whether I was the right person to write about happiness. The truth is that despite what you have read during the first week of this spiritual journey, it has been a rough old year.

I was due to move house on a bitterly cold day in February. While the removal firm was loading my furniture on to the van I had a phone call from the solicitor. I assumed that it was to confirm that I could collect the key, but in fact the message was that the company from whom I was buying the flat had gone bankrupt, and the bank had seized all the properties.

> It would be just another illusion to believe that reaching out to God will free us from pain and suffering. Often, indeed, it will take us where we would rather not go. But we know that without going there we will not find our life.
>
> *Henri Nouwen, Dutch priest and writer, 1932–96*

With the removal van taking my possessions into storage, and me on my mobile ringing round to find a place to sleep that night, I thought, 'This is the worst thing that has ever happened in my life.'

Of course, with the sense of perspective I have now, I know that it wasn't the worst thing that has happened to me. There have been bereavements and illnesses and crushing disappointments. But the pain of what we are experiencing at any one moment distorts our sense of what unhappiness really means. If we are truly honest, at its height our own toothache is worse than someone else's cancer.

That night, lying in a strange bed unable to sleep, the bitterness, gall and downcast soul of Lamentations were reality.

But can I tell you something I've learnt? It is deeply and tangibly comforting to know that people are praying alongside and for you. As Christians we are community, not individuals. At one point someone told me what time that evening he was going to pray for me, and I set the alarm on my phone so that it reminded me. Knowing that all these people had their minds open to the mind of God, and that I was their subject, was transforming. Prayer mattered during those painful months more than I can ever recall.

> True happiness is not attained through self-gratification, but through fidelity to a worthy purpose.
>
> Helen Keller, North American academic, deaf and blind from infancy, 1880–1968

Did prayer change things? I don't know what to think about that. Yesterday it rained miserably on a church fete, even though people had prayed for sun. The truth is that I don't believe a million people praying for it to be sunny would have stopped the rain. And I similarly don't think that a million people praying for that firm not to go bust would have prevented the misery. And yet . . .

And yet! Halfway through the crisis I made my daily phone call to the solicitor, who said, 'We are dealing with two financial problems. One is with Barclays Bank and that will be solved, although it will be slow. The other is with the Bank of Madagascar, which will be much more difficult.'

As you can imagine, that week God was bothered by my friends about the banks of Barclays and Madagascar more than at any time in history. Four days later, the solicitor spoke only about Barclays. I asked, 'And what about the Bank of Madagascar?' She replied, 'That doesn't appear to be a problem after all.' It is completely typical of my experience of God that, just when I have decided how he operates and what the real value of prayer is, something takes me by surprise and I am forced to think again.

> O Lord my God, help me recognize that every good thing in my life has been your gift, even when I am struggling through times of hardship.
> Amen.

In the middle of all that turmoil, which took weeks and weeks to conclude, I read the book of Lamentations. Like its writer, I asked, 'Why is God putting me through this?' My conclusion, naive and inadequate though it is, is that just as a test pilot pushes a plane to extremes – not to break it up, but to make its reliability complete – life's difficulties give me a reason to cling closer to God.

I'm in the flat. It's fine. Come and visit! This afternoon I screwed coat hooks into the wall, which is not quite as impressive as rebuilding the walls of Jerusalem, but given my DIY skills ranks as an equivalent achievement. While you are imagining me bumbling over that, I want you to give some thought to this question: are you a happy person to whom unhappy things inevitably happen from time to time? Or is the basic context of your life unhappiness, in which joyful things periodically relieve the discontent?

> Be happy!
> Will you be a happy person to whom unhappy things inevitably happen from time to time? Or will the basic context of your life be unhappiness, in which joyful things periodically relieve the discontent? You can choose.

This question is fundamental and I will revisit it over the course of this spiritual journey. It is vital because, to a very large degree, you can choose which of those is true. I'll say that again: you can choose whether you are going to be happy.

It is my prayer for you that you will decide that you are a happy person, because once you have made that choice, the reality of it can follow. And all shall be well. And all shall be well. And all manner of thing shall be well.

A happy heart

Be Happy!

Day 8

Branch out

The idea of being a community can have a bad reputation in the part of the country where I live, and I have no idea why. I've just moved into a new flat, so I've been knocking on all the doors in the block to say hallo. One of my new neighbours said, 'We've got a good group of people living here now. They all keep themselves to themselves.' Time will tell whether they think I am a good neighbour, because I have the wrong kind of temperament for keeping myself to myself!

In contrast, I went on holiday with my friend Paul to south-west Ireland. Probably my best holiday ever! It was

> [Jesus said,] 'I am the vine; you are the branches. If you remain in me and I in you, you will bear much fruit; apart from me you can do nothing. If you do not remain in me, you are like a branch that is thrown away and withers; such branches are picked up, thrown into the fire and burned. If you remain in me and my words remain in you, ask whatever you wish, and it will be given you. This is to my Father's glory, that you bear much fruit, showing yourselves to be my disciples.'
>
> *John 15.5–8*

Easter and we were staying in a bed and breakfast on the Kerry peninsular. We said to the owner, 'Can you recommend anywhere for us to eat tonight?'

She said, 'Sure now, they shouldn't really be opening because it's Good Friday, but if you go to the hotel by the beach they'll cook you something grand.'

Next morning at breakfast I said, 'Oh, by the way, we went to the restaurant you recommended.' She said, 'Sure I know you did. I've been on the phone. Which one of you had the steak and which one had the fish?'

I would hate to be caught in the middle of a scandal there. But, oh boy, wouldn't it be great to have that kind of closeness supporting you when you are in need, and rejoicing with you when you've got something to celebrate!

This is the kind of *craic* that Jesus was talking about when he compared himself to a vine and his followers to its branches. He explained it to his disciples so that they would be happy, or as he put it, 'So that your joy may be complete.' He envisaged leaving behind him a community of believers closely attached to each other; safely attached to God. A community that keeps each other good, so that scandal isn't going to scar it within. A community that is generating goodness, so that all around it people notice what's going on and are attracted.

> [Jesus said,] 'As the Father has loved me, so have I loved you. Now remain in my love. If you obey my commands, you will remain in my love, just as I have obeyed my Father's commands and remain in his love. I have told you this so that my joy may be in you and that your joy may be complete. My command is this: Love each other as I have loved you. Greater love has no-one than this, to lay down one's life for one's friends.'
>
> John 15.9–13

The branches of a vine. What a terrific image! All connected to each other; all joined to the one root; all producing fruit. Not just ordinary fruit, but good grapes for a gorgeous wine. That's us he's talking about – those who are seeking to follow the way of Jesus, gathered into some kind of local Christian community or church. Wherever you gather with a handful of Christian people, it becomes the wine-producing region of your district. You are there so that the people of your neighbourhood can be merry. Wahey!

> When the Stranger says, 'What is the meaning of this city? Do you huddle close together because you love each other?' What will you answer? 'We all dwell together to make money from each other,' or, 'This is community.'
>
> T. S. Eliot, poet, 1888–1965

Can you be a Christian all by yourself and not be part of a church or community? Well, look at it this way. Can you drink a bottle of wine all to yourself and not be part of a group sharing it? Well, you can if you're a sad old git, but what's the point? That's nothing to do with being merry; that's being drunk. It's no good to anyone, least of all you. But with Jesus as the vine and you as the branches, glorious fruit grows.

Jesus' theory was that three things would allow a cluster of believers to grow in all the ways he envisaged. The first was remaining in Jesus, the second was loving the others in the community, and the third was showing others that it works.

Remaining in Jesus means keeping open the life-giving channels between you and him that are going to make you thrive – praying, listening, praising, learning about God, talking about God. To make a habit of those turns the fact of God into a vivid reality flowing up and down you.

This morning I suddenly remembered an experiment we did at primary school. We stuck a stick of celery in a glass

43

of ink, and when we came back the next day the blue had risen up through the stalk and was coursing through the whole plant. I can't for the life of me remember what that proved! But it does remind me of the goodness of the living God coursing energetically around a human, and that is what remaining in Jesus can do for you.

Loving one another is the second aspect. And just in case anyone questions this because it sounds a bit soft-centred and frilly, Jesus goes on to explain what he has in mind by that love: 'Greater love has no one than this, to lay down one's life for one's friends.' He is talking about the same kind of love that he showed to those around him during his life. Rock-hard, sacrificial, unsentimental love – the kind that improves people's circumstances. The kind that knows what is going on in people's lives, investigates the best thing that could happen to make things better, and then puts the required effort into making that happen.

> I cannot give you a kiss, so instead the bearer of this letter is bringing you two little kegs of wine. As a mark of our love for each other, please use them for a couple of days' rejoicing with your friends.
>
> *Boniface, missionary to Germany, in a letter to Bishop Ecgbert, his friend left behind in England, 672–754*

> Lord Jesus, please give me good friends who share my determination to stay close to you. Amen.

Without moving from the window of my flat I can see the homes of three people whose lives would genuinely be improved this week by someone inviting them round for a coffee. It ought to be me, I suppose. It's not exactly laying down your life, is it? 'Greater love has no one than this, to boil up one's kettle for one's friends.' But you could start with that and see where you go next.

Jesus described showing others in the neighbourhood that following him works as 'bearing fruit'. The way he put it was: 'This is my Father's glory, that you bear much fruit, showing yourselves to be my disciples.' How will you know that you are bearing fruit? When you see that the values that make up the kingdom of God are being adopted by those next to whom you live. They are values such as peace, love, justice, tolerance, compassion.

You will know that this community of the vine is having an influence when you see that people are meeting and enjoying their neighbours, instead of grumbling about them. You will know it when you notice that the concern people have for the future of the earth is leading them to behave responsibly towards the local environment. And when you detect that people's generosity towards the poorest communities in the world is becoming greater. And when your neighbours turn out to want the best for despised members of society – asylum seekers, ex-offenders, people with personality disorders – instead of seeing them as a problem to get rid of into someone else's neighbourhood. And frankly, you will know it when you see people come to Christian faith and join us as branches of the vine.

We are a community of the vine so that others will be glad to be alive. Merry as can be! Remaining in Jesus, loving one another, showing other people it works. We can't do this by ourselves. None of us can! But in the streets around you are the resources you need to do this – like-minded fellow Christians. And within you is the Lord Jesus, who called himself the vine. Time to branch out! *Sláinte!* Cheers!

> **Be happy!**
> I can't think of a better way of responding to today's step of this spiritual journey than by opening a bottle of something luscious. But not by yourself, obviously! This is something to share in community.

45

Be Happy!

Day 9

Pass on encouragement

When I took on the job I am currently doing it was the first time I'd had a substantial managerial role. And the truth is, I didn't have a clue what I was doing. Not a scooby!

So I found myself sitting in a circle at an event for managers to discuss issues that we had in common. The facilitator of the event began by asking each of us to tell the rest of the group what we felt our management style was. And because I was sitting on her left, she said, 'Let's start with Peter, and go round the circle.'

> Encourage one another and build each other up, just as in fact you are doing … Live in peace with each other. And we urge you, brothers, warn those who are idle, encourage the timid, help the weak, be patient with everyone.
>
> *1 Thessalonians 5.11–14*

I had no idea what I was supposed to say, but I was aware of a dozen pairs of eyes looking at me, so I knew I had to say something. 'Well,' I hesitated. 'Mainly I hug people and send lots of postcards.'

The rest of the group stared at me as though this was the worst answer they had ever heard to a question on a training course.

(The reason for this was closely related to the fact that it *was* the worst answer that had ever been given to a question on a training course.)

At the end of the humiliating exercise, the facilitator was summing up, and she said: 'At the beginning, Peter told us that he has a pastoral managerial style, prioritizing affirmation and communication.'

And I thought, 'Did I? . . . Oh! . . . Yes, I suppose I did!'

I have dredged up that embarrassing story about my job (which I may no longer have if my boss has read this chapter) both because I was immensely encouraged by the facilitator helping me to see what I do intuitively as having professional merit, and because it made me determined to go on making encouragement central to my relationships at work.

From the very early days of Christianity, even before it was known by that name, encouragement was seen as one of the most important factors in the relationship between the followers of Jesus. In fact, one of the first leaders of the church was a man called Joseph, who came from Cyprus. He showed that quality so intensely that the men who had been with Jesus nicknamed him 'The Encourager'. It stuck so firmly that although he is mentioned many times in the New Testament, the writers never call him by his real name but use his nickname instead: Barnabas (which in Aramaic means something like 'fathered by encouragement').

> I pray that you may be active in sharing your faith, so that you will have a full understanding of every good thing we have in Christ. Your love has given me great joy and encouragement, because you, brother, have refreshed the hearts of the saints.
>
> *Philemon 1.6–7*

It was an act of sizeable generosity that earned Barnabas

his name, but his way with people proved that he deserved it again and again. He knew how to take someone's side when no one else was doing so. Paul felt the benefit of his encouragement when the rest of the Christians in Jerusalem were afraid that his dramatic conversion to the way of Jesus was a trick to betray them. Mark knew the benefit when, after he had messed up an opportunity to serve Jesus, Barnabas took him under his wing and gave him a second chance.

Courage is at the hub of encouragement – literally in the middle of the word, and practically at the heart of the action. Encouragement gives people the bravery to be the best they could be. It lifts people's spirits and makes them feel that they are doing something with genuine worth. No wonder it was so important to the Christians in the first church, where it often took real courage to maintain a new set of beliefs and values. So here is a practical course in how to be encouraging, step by ascending step.

> One of the most beautiful gifts in the world is the gift of encouragement. When someone encourages you, that person helps you over a threshold you might otherwise never have crossed on your own.
>
> *John O'Donohue, priest and philosopher, 1956–2008*

First of all, smile at people. It takes barely any effort, but it is one of the simplest ways of increasing happiness, especially if the person is a stranger and you have only one chance to make a positive impact on them.

Second, listen to people properly. It seems simplistic to say it, but people so often feel that they have not been understood. Just fixing your eye on someone and showing that you have heard what they are saying is immensely encouraging. At a party last Saturday I was tempted to tell the person I was trying to chat to that the fact that he kept looking over my shoulder to see whether someone more interesting had come into the room behind me was doing nothing to add to my enjoyment of the evening.

Then start to use words. The invention of text messaging has been a godsend for those who are naturally inclined to be encouragers, because it is perfect for the eight-letter-long message which is too short for a phone call or letter – 'well done' or 'thank you'. Whether a message of encouragement is spoken or written, short or long, makes no discernible difference. The thing that makes the difference is that someone bothered.

> Those who bring sunshine into the lives of others cannot keep it from themselves.
>
> J. M. Barrie, playwright, 1860–1937

And at the top of this ladder of encouragement come actions. That can mean practical help, which is immensely heartening for obvious reasons. It can mean offering a gift (and it is the warmth of the thought that is the encouraging element, not the cost of the present). It can involve spending time, which is extremely affirming. And, of course, it can be expressed with touch. (Oh please! Don't deliberately misunderstand me! I'm talking about unobtrusive and wholesome ways of touching people, not throwing unwilling acquaintances on to the floor and snogging them.)

> Lord God, whenever I am next to a person whose life would be enriched by some encouragement, give me a nudge and show me what to do.
> Amen.

When the impetus at the heart of all these actions is kindness, people's circumstances improve. 'Give, and it will be given to you,' said Jesus. That is not the motive, but it is surely the result!

Here is a challenge that I believe will increase the amount

of basic happiness in the world! Set out to leave every person you meet with a life that is minutely better than it was before they came into contact with you. This not the same as just being nice to people, which is a basic human duty. Instead, it is a conscious effort to imagine yourself into the life of the person with whom you are interacting, and work out how your presence in it can be a force for good. With people you know well, such as work colleagues, monitor whether having an attitude like that changes your behaviour towards them. To do it day after day will require an effort, but its impact could be thrilling. With people you meet for just a few seconds, such as a waitress or a bus conductor, it requires even more imagination and quick thinking. But if you pit your wits at this as if it were a game, the fun is infectious! What would make that person glad they served you? (You must be able to think of something more inventive than just leaving a tip!)

In the New Testament, Paul wrote often about the importance of Christians encouraging one another. In particular he urged those who were in positions of responsibility to take advantage of the opportunity they have been given to build people's confidence, strength and joy. He knew that in giving these things, greater blessings would be received in return. He described the process as 'refreshing the hearts of the saints'. We could all do with a spot of that!

> **Be happy!**
> Set yourself the task during the coming week of leaving every person with whom you interact with a life that is fractionally better because of meeting you.

Incidentally, you remember that group of managers in front of whom I embarrassed myself? I am happy to report that at the end of the course one of them hugged me, and the next week two of them sent me postcards. So I must have said something right!

Be Happy!

Day 10

Be generous

Researchers have been at work to try to explain one of the paradoxes of modern life – that increasing wealth does not necessarily make people happier. In 2008, academic psychologists at the University of British Columbia in Vancouver, Canada, published a study in the journal *Science* which seems to suggest that how people spend their money is every bit as important as how much of it they have in the first place.

There were three parts to their research. First they interviewed 632 American men and women and discovered that the regularity with which they spent money on other people was a strong indicator of their general level of happiness.

Next they studied sixteen individuals who were employed by a company in Boston, Massachusetts, knowing

> Command those who are rich in this present world not to be arrogant nor to put their hope in wealth, which is so uncertain, but to put their hope in God, who richly provides us with everything for our enjoyment. Command them to do good, to be rich in good deeds, and to be generous and willing to share. In this way they will lay up treasure for themselves.
>
> 1 Timothy 6.17–19

that they were about to receive an unexpected bonus of several thousand dollars. They interviewed the workers before they heard the news, without revealing why, and then spoke to the same people two months later. They compiled a league table of happiness levels, and discovered that a clear pattern emerged. The more of the bonus that the employees devoted to what the researchers called 'pro-social' spending (that is, generosity to good causes, friends, needy people or schemes to improve the world), the higher they found themselves on the chart of happiness.

Finally, the researchers gave forty-six student volunteers an envelope containing either five dollars or twenty dollars in cash. They gave them instructions to spend it by that afternoon, either on themselves or on others. Questioned at the end of the day, those who spent it on others reported feelings of happiness greater than those who spent it on themselves. And it seems that the amount of money involved makes no difference – even a small act of generosity can increase the level of happiness you feel on any given day.

> One gives freely, yet gains even more; another withholds unduly, but comes to poverty. A generous person will prosper; the one who refreshes others will be refreshed. People curse those who hoard grain, but blessing crowns those who are willing to sell.
>
> *Proverbs 11.24–26*

I don't think these results would have surprised Jesus! 'When you give to the needy,' he said, 'do not announce it with trumpets. Do not let your left hand know what your right hand is doing, so that your giving may be in secret. Then your Father, who sees what is done in secret, will reward you.' What kind of reward? A life that is richer and more contented, despite a wallet that is emptier. I love that idea – secretly and subversively making someone else's life better.

These are the words of Professor Elizabeth Dunn, who organized the research: 'Although real incomes have surged dramatically in recent decades, happiness levels have remained largely flat in developed countries across time. One of the most intriguing explanations for this counter-intuitive finding is that people often pour their increased wealth into pursuits that provide little in the way of lasting happiness, such as purchasing costly consumer goods.' If I shut my eyes I can imagine St Paul saying that. If he were alive. Or Canadian. Or a psychologist. Or a professor. Or female.

> I don't know what your destiny will be, but one thing I know: The only ones among you who will be truly happy are those who will have sought and found how to serve.
>
> *Albert Schweitzer, Nobel prize-winning doctor and missionary, 1875–1965*

There is a strange irony at work in the human soul, which emerged as part of the experiment. The thought of gaining or having money makes people less likely to want to help acquaintances, donate to charity, or even spend time generously with others. But those are, in fact, the very acts that are likely to make people happy. It is as though we need someone to speak sharply to us to make us come to our senses. Perhaps that is why Paul was so assertive when he gave advice

> Over the years those who have seemed to me to be the most happy, contented and fulfilled have always been the people who have lived the most outgoing and unselfish lives. I hope that, like me, you will be comforted by the example of Jesus of Nazareth who, often in circumstances of great adversity, managed to live a generous and sacrificial life.
>
> *HM Queen Elizabeth II, born 1926*

to Timothy in one of his letters: 'Command those who are rich in this present world not to be arrogant nor to put their hope in wealth.' And as always, he gave a good reason: 'Wealth is so uncertain, but they should put their hope in God, who richly provides us with everything for our enjoyment.' That is the reason for being generous. Not because we can only please God when we have become truly miserable, but because a big-hearted, open-handed approach to life is the most enjoyable way to get through it.

This is the God who has been so generous towards humankind that it led Paul to blurt out, 'Thanks be to God for his unspeakable gift!' Jesus. I suppose I have always thought that God must have screwed up his emotions with great determination and sorrowfully let Jesus go from his presence into a needy world. But the Canadian research has put a new thought into my head about God's staggeringly gracious gift. Perhaps he knew from eternity what giving Jesus to the world would mean, and was beside himself with happiness at the prospect of being able to lavish his generosity on men and women. Perhaps, like my godchildren, God just couldn't wait for the first Christmas to arrive!

> God my great benefactor, I can't stand the thought of being a shrivelled-up and resentful giver. Teach me true generosity – the kind that genuinely rejoices to know that others are happy. Amen.

Paul's counsel to his Christian friends gets more and more insistent: 'Be rich in good deeds. Be generous and willing to share.' It is a beautiful thought that threads its way all through the Bible. One thousand years earlier, one of the wise men of Israel captured its wisdom in a proverb: 'A generous person will prosper; the one who refreshes others will be refreshed.' No scientific research there, I guess – just an insightful observation of life. And he goes on:

'People curse those who hoard grain, but blessing crowns those who are willing to sell.' The wise man must have looked out at the harvest fields on a glorious summer day. He knew that farmers were hoarding grain knowing that, when shortages came during the winter months, they could bump up their prices and make a big profit. God's attitude was: 'That may be good business, but it's a rotten plan for a fulfilled life. Better to be generous and loved than rich and isolated.'

I don't know about your home town, but here in Croydon we don't hoard much grain. However, I have been trying to think of equivalent ways of being generous. Would you be able to join me in a month of living generously, between now and the end of this forty-day spiritual journey? Can we together be as inventive as possible in devising ways to give?

I challenge you to think of ideas that will improve the lives of friends (such as baking a sponge for someone who has never seen a cake that didn't come wrapped in plastic from Tesco); or improve the lives of strangers (such as planting bulbs in public places). Some may be gifts to needy people (such as donating clothes to a project for homeless men and women); others may be gifts to a needy planet (such as turning off electrical appliances that are on standby). You could direct some at humans (such as transferring your savings to an ethical account), but others you could direct at God himself (such as lovingly singing a hymn of praise in the privacy of your own bedroom).

> **Be happy!**
> Randomly commit some acts of generosity to total strangers for no apparent reason – just so that the amount of happiness in the world rises by a tiny degree. Do it anonymously and enjoy thinking about the pleasure it will give. You can find some ideas at www.generous.org.uk.

Actually, all of them are investments in your own happiness, as Paul, the ancient wise men, and the modern psychologists seem to agree. But the inspiration for every one of them is the gracious love of God – that generous, bighearted, open-handed love of which there is so much for you and me that passing it on is a joy.

Be Happy!
Day 11
Risk being loved

Prostitutes are always treated with extraordinary compassion in the Bible.

That kind of opening sentence usually gets people's attention! I have reread all the Bible stories about prostitution, after visiting a project in the red light district of a city in the north of England run by a remarkable Christian woman known as Sue. As I heard the tragic stories of people for whom this degrading and dangerous life is the only option for survival, many of my presuppositions were overturned. I found myself thinking, 'This person is not a sinner; she is someone who has been sinned against.' Thank God that a project such as Sue's exists, offering the acceptance, self-esteem and care that can make different opportunities possible.

> 'In that day,' declares the Lord,
> 'you will call me "my husband";
> you will no longer call me "my master" ...
> I will betroth you to me for ever;
> I will betroth you in righteousness and justice,
> in love and compassion.
> I will betroth you in faithfulness,
> and you will acknowledge the Lord.'
>
> *Hosea 2.16, 19, 20*

And that is precisely the kind of attitude that the Bible has. Rahab, the common prostitute, finds herself one of the ancestors of Jesus. Esther, the high-class prostitute, is lauded as the rescuer of her people. Mary is so transformed by Jesus that she becomes one of the first witnesses to the resurrection. And in the book of Hosea comes the story of Gomer, to whom God promises healing, restoration and a place in his presence.

I presume that Gomer was a real person. Her story is like that of a million others in each generation from the eighth century BC to this very day. Hosea marries. His wife Gomer yearns for something else and leaves. She uses sex to fill the gap – financial, emotional, spiritual – that is left. Love has made Hosea so desperate to have her back that he pays for his own wife's prostitution services. He pleads for her to make a new start and to be faithful to him. And the end of the story? Who knows! The Bible keeps us guessing.

The only reason why anyone would wonder whether she was a real person is that she stands for so much in the story. It is an allegory in which every character represents something bigger. Gomer's name means 'It's all over', which must have been her last words to

> [Hosea said,] 'Come, let us return to the Lord.
> He has torn us to pieces,
> but he will heal us;
> he has injured us,
> but he will bind up our wounds.
> After two days he will revive us;
> on the third day he will restore us,
> that we may live in his presence.
> Let us acknowledge the Lord;
> let us press on to acknowledge him.
> As surely as the sun rises, he will appear;
> he will come to us like the winter rains,
> like the spring rains that water the earth.'
>
> *Hosea 6.1–3*

> Do not keep accounts with our Lord. Go bankrupt! Let our Lord love you without justice. Say frankly, 'He loves me because I do not deserve it; that is the wonderful thing about him. And that is why I, in my turn, love him as well as I can without worrying whether I deserve to be allowed to love him' ... Come then! Show a little deference to our Lord, and allow him to go first. Let him love you a great deal, a very great deal, long before you have succeeded in loving him even a little.
>
> *Henri de Tourville, French priest and writer, 1842–1903*

Hosea before she left. Hosea's name means 'God will save' and it is a variation on that popular Hebrew name shared by Joshua, Jesse and, of course, Jesus. In the story, Hosea stands for God, and Gomer for God's people, going away from him again and again. Out of his great love, God never loses hope in the possibility of the return of the nations, the people, the individuals whom he adores.

The names of the children born to Hosea and Gomer represent the despair that the family had sunk to, and the desolation of Israel many centuries before Jesus. Hosea named them 'No one loves you' and 'Nothing to do with me'. I suppose that's the reason why part of me hopes that these were not real people, but symbols, because the burden of being cursed from birth with names such as those must have been intolerable.

But that, frankly, was the mess that Israel was in. If you want a snapshot of the chaos, all you need to know is that Jeroboam, the king at the time of Hosea,

> Let the love of God be stronger than death in you.
>
> *John of Apamea, Syrian monk, about 400–50*

was Israel's sixth king in twenty years, and all but one of them assassinated his predecessor. A whole generation of children had grown up not worshipping God. Instead they had become intimate with the idols and gods of nations with whom Israel had sought disastrous political alliances. Prostitution is a good metaphor for what they were doing. Disappointment with God had led them to abandon him and try to fill the gap in their lives – financial, emotional, spiritual – elsewhere.

In that setting the book of Hosea is a book of urging, warning, pleading, promising, forgiving – all the things that Hosea did out of love of his wife, and that God did for Israel. And, scarcely credible though it is, that God does for you and me.

The fact that the writer of Hosea refuses to tell us the end of the story is utterly frustrating. Wrongdoing had infiltrated every part of the way that God's people related to him, to each other, and to the rest of the world. And God was about to bring things to a head. The last warning had been given. The last pleading. Come back to Hosea. Come back to God. We hear Gomer sighing, 'Let us return to the Lord. He has torn us to pieces but he will heal us; he has injured us but he will bind up our wounds.'

Surely we can expect a happy ending. Surely there is going to be a reconciliation. I have always imagined that after those words came a long, long pause in the conversation between Hosea and Gomer. There must have been a pause, because Hosea would have been wondering what on earth he should do. All his friends would have been advising him, 'Don't do it! Don't take her back! Are you mad? She's worthless. You have remained holy, but she has let you down. And she'll let you down again. Don't do it!'

> Lord God, I have absolutely no idea what I have done that would make you want to love me. And I understand even less why you require so little from me in return. All I can say is that, humbly and gratefully, I acknowledge you. Come bind up my wounds.
> Amen.

And Hosea breaks in, 'I know, I know, I know, I know, I know . . . but . . . I love her. What else can I possibly do?'

I (and, unless I have completely misjudged the situation, you too) have times in life when I reach the crunch point at which I know that I have done wrong and that the holy God should, if he has any sense, reject me as worthless. And I can imagine all the advice that could conceivably be given to God: 'Don't do it! Don't take him back. He'll let you down again.' And God breaks in, 'I know, I know, I know . . . but . . . I love him. I love her. I love human beings. What else can I possibly do?'

What should I do in response to this undeserved and overwhelming love? What can I do out of gratitude? I could pray. I could endure all kinds of boring church services. I could make all sorts of sacrifices.

> **Be happy!**
> Take a risk in letting God love you and see whether it makes you happy. Make a decision to stop worrying about something and trust that a loving God will take care of it. Pray about something you have never mentioned before. Write the Lord a love letter. Tell someone that you worship God. See what happens!

'No, no!' replies God. 'It's very nice of you to offer, but it's not what matters. All I want is for you to risk being loved by me.'

Risk being loved by God! Or as the writer of the book of Hosea puts it: 'Let us acknowledge the Lord; let us press on to acknowledge him.'

Surely it can't be that simple! But it is. The writer goes on: 'On the third day he will restore us, that we may live in his presence.' The third day. The resurrection day. The day of life.

Gomer. The people of God. 'It's all over.'

Hosea. Jesus. 'God will save.' Alleluia!

Be Happy!

Day 12

Make a difference

Joni caught my attention because I'm always drawn to naughty boys with a twinkle in their eye. Joni is ten and he is Haitian. But he lives across the border of that Caribbean island in the Dominican Republic. I went to his school, which is funded by Christian Aid through money that you, or people like you, have given.

It was lunchtime and the school was serving a meal. The children shut their eyes and put their hands together to say grace. The words they say each day are: 'There is nothing better than shared bread, and a life of love shared every day. God bless this bread with goodness; God bless our lives with solidarity.' I knew what a terrific image children praying would be, so I lifted my camera and, just as I did, Joni opened his eyes wide and stuck his thumbs in the corners of his mouth to make a cheeky grin.

> On this mountain the Lord Almighty will prepare a feast of rich food for all peoples ... the best of meats and the finest of wines. On this mountain he will ... swallow up death for ever. The Sovereign Lord will wipe away the tears from all faces; he will remove this disgrace from all the earth.
>
> Isaiah 25.6–8

62

Flash! Brilliant mischievous photo! I knew I wanted to hear his story.

I worked for Christian Aid for several years, and one of my jobs was to choose the photographs that go on posters for display in churches. Truly, I did not want to show photographs of children suffering in distress. I know that poverty is an absolutely dreadful thing and that millions of people live in conditions that no human being should have to tolerate. But that's not the whole of the story.

When I think back, the images I recall from the developing world are women bent double in the fields working astonishingly hard while babies sleep, strapped to their backs. Or children giggling on their way to school in uniforms so crisp that they put my neighbours to shame. Or water being carried from a well with great skill on a young girl's head. Or the generosity shown by the poorest people in the world in delight that someone has flown so far to meet them. Or the hilarity caused by me protecting myself with sun block when, as people invariably pointed out, I'm quite white enough already. They are not images of despair; they are images of life.

> [Jesus prayed,] 'Your Kingdom come, your will be done on earth as it is in heaven.'
>
> Matthew 6.10

It was a quandary because I'm sure that photos of starving children would make people empty their wallets to give them food. But repeatedly those in the developing world told me that they do not want handouts. They want a platform on which to stand so that they can work hard, earn a reasonable wage, get better when they are sick, and find their own way

> I refuse to study books made from dead skin while people are dying of hunger.
>
> Dominic, founder of the Dominican religious order, 1170–1221

63

out of poverty. Actually, that's pretty much what I want from life as well. Except that it's easy for me to have those ambitions; how on earth do you achieve them if you earn seventy pence a day? It is so unfair.

So Joni, God bless him, leads me down a mud path to his home in the shadow of a derelict sugar factory. On the way he's cracking jokes, and telling me that he wants to be a builder, and how it's not right that he had to wash the dishes that day when it's his sister's turn. It is all so like chatting to my godchildren that I half expect to turn the corner and see a neat house with a privet hedge. So it's a shock when we arrive.

It's made of corrugated iron, it has no electricity or running water, and the whole family lives in two rooms. The house is by a river, which floods without warning three or four times a year bringing water into the house up to a metre high. They have to grab what they can and scamper up the hill, where they stay with a relative until the water subsides. Joni tells me this completely cheerfully, and his teacher explains that these families really need to move to better housing, but because they are Haitian, not Dominican, they have no legal rights in the Dominican Republic. They can get only the worst-paid jobs, and have no entitlement to health care or education. All the time I'm thinking, 'Oh Joni, I'm so sorry, I am so sorry.' But he's just saying, 'Will you take my photo now?'

> If I can't subtract from the world's sum of misery, do I have to add to it personally? It's one of those questions I mean to take up if ever I get religion.
>
> P. J. O'Rourke, North American satirist, born 1947

In the middle of this fearfully poor, grey community there is a great pink sign of hope. It's a school, and it is run by a marvellous organization called Onè Respè. In some ways it is like any primary school in the UK – on the day I visited, the class was learning subtraction. But it's free, so it's the only way Haitians can get an education. And children get their only substantial meal of the day there.

The lady who cooks is called Matola. There are 129 children and I asked Matola how much it would cost to feed the whole school lunch. She did some sums and I worked out the exchange rate. We reckon it costs £9 to feed them all rice pudding and banana. I explained to her that £9 is about the amount people think of giving when they see a charity collecting box, so it would be good for them to know that their contribution would buy a day's food for a whole school. A beam spread across her face and she said, 'Wait a moment!' She did some more sums and announced, 'On treat days we give them bread and butter with chocolate spread. That would cost £15.'

> God bless our bread with goodness; God bless our lives with solidarity.
> Amen.

I originally thought that I couldn't possibly ask people to give £6 extra so that children can have chocolate. But on the plane home I thought, hey, why not! Why not give children in a poor country a treat? It's the sort of thing I do all the time for my godchildren. I don't just want the children of the developing world to survive; I want them to live!

Jacqui Abreu is Joni's head teacher. I asked her what his prospects are. I get the impression that although Joni is charming, he is not the brightest of the bunch. But she told me that he would grow up knowing from his earliest years that no matter what his skin colour, or whether he is rich or poor, he is a creature of God, treated with all the dignity that a human being deserves. 'Don't underestimate that!' she said.

Together, Jacqui and I read a Bible passage from Isaiah about heaven. I asked her what she thought heaven will be like. 'Heaven!' she said exuberantly. 'I've dreamt about heaven repeatedly. In my dream there is a calm place with people sitting. I hear myself saying, "This can't be heaven; heaven is supposed to be different from earth." I see a lot of poor people and poor homes. I feel I need nothing that I haven't already got. Although the houses are poor, there is no feeling of need. Things go easily, with no one hungry or thirsty. And the fields are just like the ones near here. In fact, heaven could be right here – but without the problems.'

Can I tell you something I realized yesterday evening? I have never once in my life had a day at the end of which I was hungry. Not once! It had been a complicated day, and the result was that when I sat down to write this chapter at nine o'clock I'd had nothing to eat. Halfway through I realized I was hungry, so I went to the kitchen and fetched an apple. As I typed with one finger and the apple in the other hand, I thought: 'This is what comfort means in South London. I'm hungry, so I walk twenty paces knowing that in two minutes' time I won't be.' How do you say thank you to God for that?

> **Be happy!**
> Make a donation to a charity that helps the world's poorest people to work their way out of poverty.

It's *ludicrously* fortunate. And how do you live with yourself, sitting in front of a computer, instant food in hand, when there are 1.6 billion people in the world hoping to survive the night in absolute poverty?

I got myself a bit dejected after that. But this morning here I am, finishing the story. And next to me is a photo of Joni, grinning like a crescent moon. And I'm thinking, 'Well, we are not powerless to make a difference. We know what needs to be done.'

So go, Joni, go! Thousands of people have read your story now. You're famous – I bet you never thought that was possible! You have become God's messenger. I hope you're not hungry today. I hope we won't let you down.

Be Happy!
Day 13
Find your place

I've just bought a new iron. Steam iron – nice one! I read
the instructions because I wanted to understand the symbols. They included: 'Warning – do not iron clothes while
they are being worn.' Do you know, that would never have
occurred to me until I read the leaflet!

On Friday I mentioned this to one of my friends. She gig-
gled: 'Look at this, then!' She went upstairs and brought
down her little boy's Superman outfit. The label in the

In Damascus there was a disciple named Ananias. The Lord
called to him in a vision, 'Ananias!' 'Yes, Lord,' he answered.
The Lord told him, 'Go to the house of Judas on Straight
Street and ask for a man from Tarsus named Saul [Paul], for
he is praying. In a vision he has seen a man named Ananias
come and place his hands on him to restore his sight.'
'Lord,' Ananias answered, 'I have heard many reports about
this man and all the harm he has done to your saints in
Jerusalem. And he has come here with authority from the
chief priests to arrest all who call on your name.' But the
Lord said to Ananias, 'Go! This man is my chosen instrument
to carry my name before the Gentiles.'

Acts 9.10–15

collar read: 'Caution – dressing in this costume does not enable the wearer to fly.'

The reason I am telling you this is that I know, I absolutely know, that I will never be St Paul. Some people will be like St Paul because that is the gift that God has put in them – some people reading this book, possibly. I guess I would have liked that gift, but I haven't got it. I could wear the costume, but I would never fly. And that's that!

God had an almighty task for Paul to do. A herald was needed for a pioneering missionary enterprise – to announce that Jesus was God, walking and talking on the earth. So God chose a new convert. He chose a man of immense intellectual stature. He chose someone with rigorous moral integrity. He chose someone with great physical stamina. He chose someone with a testimony that an encounter with Jesus can be completely transforming. Today God still uses people with those qualities, but I know I don't have them.

> Stand firm. Let nothing move you. Always give yourselves fully to the work of the Lord, because you know that your labour in the Lord is not in vain.
>
> *I Corinthians 15.58*

Paul had been present when, for the first time, a follower of Jesus was put to death in a barbaric way. I think he may have imagined that this would put an end to the new sect, and certainly the followers of Jesus scattered. The unexpected thing was that they scattered like a forest fire scatters, igniting new communities of faith wherever they went.

With the church growing, Paul obtained the documents he needed to authorize the persecution of the Christians. Under Roman military control, the jurisdiction of the Jewish leaders in Jerusalem did not cover them for business in Damascus. Paul had to get authority to go to Damascus, arrest the Christians, and transport them back to be tried in Jerusalem, the place where they had committed the so-called offences. That's how he ended up rattling down the road, arrest warrants in hand, cursing the Christians whom he thought were impeding God's plan for the world.

> God has created me to do some definite service; he has committed some work to me which he has not committed to another. I have my mission – I may never know it in this life, but I shall be told it in the next. I am a link in a chain, a bond of connection between persons. He has not created me for naught. I shall do good. I shall do his work. I shall be an angel of peace, a preacher of truth in my own place while not intending it, if I do but keep his commandments. Therefore I will trust him.
>
> John Henry Newman, cardinal, 1801–90

And bang! The most famous conversion in Christian history took place. When Paul later described what happened, he wrote, 'The Lord Jesus arrested me.' (Actually, he didn't put it quite like that. He said, 'Jesus took hold of me.' But the irony is still there.) Temporarily blinded, he was led to a place where he had to rely on strangers to keep him alive, so he had nothing else to turn to but prayer. I wonder what he said to God during those frightening days.

That's what it took for God to take someone who had all the right skills, pluck him out of what he was doing, and set him on the route to being the greatest evangelist of history. It's not going to happen to me. I will never be Paul.

I might . . . I might one day be Ananias. We forget that he is part of Paul's story. He had a vision from God too. It wasn't so dramatic but, my goodness, it was just as important. At this point the Lord was relying for the future of the entire kingdom of God not on Paul, who was a confused, feeble mess praying for help. Instead, the future of

69

Christianity depended on a rather insignificant believer who, not long ago, had fled for his life from Jerusalem and was now taking shelter in Damascus. It was Ananias who was actually going to change history.

Sensitive! That's the first thing I want to say about Ananias. To be sensitive to God is a real skill. It's one that everyone can develop, but it doesn't come effortlessly. It requires you to be asking continually, 'What might God be wanting me to learn through this?' As you open a newspaper, as situations unfold at work, as you have conversations with friends and strangers,

> For the fulfilment of his purpose, God needs more than priests, bishops, pastors and missionaries. He needs mechanics and chemists, gardeners and street sweepers, dressmakers and cooks, tradesmen, physicians, philosophers, judges and shorthand typists.
>
> *Paul Tournier, Swiss doctor, 1898–1986*

asking, 'What has this brought into my life that wasn't there before?' Of course, most of the time the things God tells us are quite insignificant. But such is the way he works in our world that we never know which the significant ones are. God needed Ananias to visit Paul. We know what a world-changing impact it had, but I'll bet Ananias didn't.

Another quality of Ananias is that he was obedient to God. I've lost count of the number of times when I have thought to myself, 'I must send an email to so-and-so,' and then never got round to doing it. I dread to think how that might frustrate God's plan for each human. I am quite sure that God is continually picking up the situation

> Loving God, I know that you have made me what I am so that I can help make the world what you want it to be. Show me my place in your plan. Amen.

when we have frustrated his plan, and creating a new alternative to bring about his good ends. Maybe if Ananias had gone to the shops instead of visiting Paul someone else would have done it. Maybe not! Who's to know? But the fact is that Ananias did the obedient thing, and the world changed.

Of course, Ananias was also immensely courageous. To go to a man who was intending to destroy you and wish him the blessing of God requires true bravery. But all those things – sensitivity, obedience, courage – could have been meaningless if it weren't for the thing I most like about Ananias. He was truly compassionate. I'm not sure whether he met Jesus in person or heard about him from others. However, he had certainly absorbed the way of Jesus into his own behaviour. What else could possibly have given him the compassion to go to a man who had been trying to imprison him and call him, 'brother'? It took remarkable inner resources. In each generation there is a need for believers who stand out as compassionate, as Jesus was, to those whom even other Christians see as part of the problem. Who will go to ex-offenders, to economic migrants, to Muslims, to homosexuals, and call them 'brother'? I plan to. You?

> **Be happy!**
> Is there anything that you are doing for which you are clearly not suited – driven to it by guilt, duty or a sense that what you do for God only pleases him if it makes you miserable? Make arrangements to stop doing it. Instead think about what delights you to do, and work out how you could use those talents to enrich God's world.

So where do you fit into this story? Intellectual, morally rigorous, entrepreneur. Go and be Paul! Put on that costume and fly! I know I can't be like you, but I wish you God's blessing, because the world needs you.

Sensitive, obedient, courageous, compassionate. Go and be Ananias! It's you who quietly give the people like Paul the energy to do what they do.

Know your place! Work out what tasks in God's world fit the skills you have and take action gladly. Happiness will follow as you realize that you are God's own, doing what only you could do.

A happy attitude

Be Happy!
Day 14
Make peace

The world is getting better, and nobody quite knows why.

In 1992 there were thirty-six wars being fought in the world. Now there are about twenty. We sometimes look at the news and think everything in the world is getting progressively worse, mainly because so many soldiers from our country are involved in conflict. But our experience skews the picture, and the fact is that there is a great deal to be encouraged by.

> Come and see the works of the Lord,
> the desolations he has brought on the earth.
> He makes wars cease to the ends of the earth;
> he breaks the bow and shatters the spear,
> he burns the shields with fire.
> 'Be still, and know that I am God;
> I will be exalted among the nations,
> I will be exalted in the earth.'
>
> *Psalm 46.8–10*

Should we be nonchalant about this? Of course not! One conflict in the world is one too many. But it does mean that next time some old codger at the bus stop rants about how the whole world is going to the dogs, you can smile because you know something that he doesn't. Good things are happening in our world. It is sustained

75

A HAPPY ATTITUDE

by a God whose heart is full of mercy and set on bringing life in all its fullness to his creation.

What are we going to do in response to the care of a good God? Three thousand years ago a Hebrew songwriter insisted that when we see war coming to an end, the only logical response is to stop everything and acknowledge the might of the Lord: 'Be still and know that I am God.'

Let me tell you about one of the world's hopeful places – Angola. In 2000 the United Nations described Angola as the worst place in the world to be a child. There had been civil war for forty years, and two generations of children had known nothing else. But in 2002 the leader of one side was killed. With him gone, everyone was too exhausted to go on fighting, so peace broke out through sheer inability to keep the hatred alive.

> The wisdom that comes from heaven is first of all pure; then peace-loving, considerate, submissive, full of mercy and good fruit, impartial and sincere. Peacemakers who sow in peace raise a harvest of righteousness.
>
> James 3.17–18

During the violence millions of people had been uprooted from their homes and fled to places of relative safety, particularly from the villages to the cities. At the end of the war the capital, Luanda, had eight times the number of people it had at the beginning. But it didn't have eight times the quantity of water or housing. The

> Let us run toward the goal which from the beginning has been handed down to us – the goal which is peace. And let us fix our gaze on the Father and Creator of the whole universe, and cling to his splendid and superlative gift of peace.
>
> Pope Clement, fourth Bishop of Rome, about 30–99

conditions were terrible and there was great poverty. So people began to think about returning to their villages.

Now, put yourself in the position of a former resident of a village who has survived a war and is thinking about going home. It takes a huge amount of courage. For a start it is a place you left in terror, so just recalling that is distressing. But also you're not sure what will still be there. Will the soldiers have burnt everything to the ground? Will there be any way to make a living?

Of course, help is available. When you get there, charities give you sacks of seeds so that you can start farming again. But that in itself brings a dilemma. Because when you arrive at the village after walking for a week, you are *very* hungry. You look at those sacks and think to yourself: 'That's three days' worth of meals there – I could feed those to my children.' So you have to decide: 'Am I going to sow the seeds and wait for a harvest to multiply them in six months' time, or am I going to have supper?' Don't underestimate what an act of faith it is to put those seeds in the ground, because it is a commitment to staying there for six months, and that requires confidence that violence will not drive you away again.

Thousands of families in Angola have returned to their villages, and organizations such as Tearfund and Christian Aid have been supporting them in their courageous decision to start all over again from scratch. Through local organizations, they have distributed seeds and tools. And they have been putting roofs back on the schools, which is also an investment in peace, because if children grow up

> Give us, O God, the vision which can see thy love in the world in spite of human failure. Show us what each one of us can do to set forth the coming of the day of universal peace.
>
> *Frank Borman, spoken from Apollo 8 while orbiting the moon on Christmas Eve 1968, born 1928*

able to read and write they can start careers, so there are better ways of being sure where the next meal is coming from than joining a rebel army.

I know all this because my friend Simeon visited Angola to see it happening, and he met Eduardo Palanga, who is thirteen. Eduardo is part of the first generation of Angolans in our lifetime that is thriving instead of declining. Simeon asked him questions he thought would interest children in this country, such as, 'Do you have any toys?'

Eduardo said, 'Yes, I have one.' He disappeared off cheerfully, and I think Simeon expected him to come back with a football. But he came back with an elastic band.

> Lord God, make me
> still enough to know
> that you are God. And
> in the stillness, set my
> heart on peace.
> Amen.

In Angola they play a game called *pisto*. You flick an elastic band against a wall, and it bounces back down into the dust. Then your friend flicks his, and if it lands on top of yours, he gets to keep it. Eduardo is evidently useless at this game, because he is down to his last elastic band. (In fact he's got two now, because Simeon gave him the one that was holding his papers together.)

Simeon was telling me this over coffee one morning, and I suddenly became ever so upset. This is the reality of poverty – that somewhere in the world there is a child whose entire toy collection is a single rubber band. I was comparing my godchildren – they have so many toys that when it comes to Christmas I honestly don't know what to give them. I don't get tearful about these things every day, because if I did I'd never get any work done. But that day I did.

I am writing this because it would be easy to produce a book about being happy without ever mentioning that we live in a world where there is immense suffering inflicted by some humans upon others. That would be useless. Most of the time I'm poised between two attitudes. I am full of hope, because the work of the charities that allow us to contribute to making the world more just and more peaceful is truly impressive. I worked for one of them for a decade, and I have seen that what you and I give transforms people's circumstances. But I also get very sad about the reality of conflict and its aftermath. It's hunger, and it's fear about what the future will hold, and it's Eduardo making do with an elastic band for his entertainment. And it is at that point, poised between the two, that I hear the Bible's call to put a different kind of seed into the ground: 'Peacemakers who sow in peace raise a harvest of righteousness.'

How do you do that? By supporting Christian Aid or Tearfund or whichever is your favourite charity, of course. But it is also done by recognizing that the lines of conflict that scar the world lie across each of our hearts as well. If the world is to continue becoming less violent, the responsibility to make that happen lies with you and me. That is why Jesus gave his blessing to peacemakers, because he knew that they are not just those standing between enemy armies in Kashmir or the Congo, but those who, in their own families and streets, decide to forsake the old battles and make a new start.

> **Be happy!**
> Find an elastic band and put it round your wrist. (My postman drops a red one outside my front door every weekday, so recycling it will be a pleasure.) Keep it on until bedtime, and let it remind you to think about the conflicts that unsettle your life, petty or major, and about what it would require to address them.

Your life and Eduardo's are joined in more ways than you can imagine. Your generosity can make him happy, and his example can make you happy. Both of you can know the blessing of being a peacemaker. Return to the village where you were once content. Sow some new seeds. Build a new roof. Be still and know that God is God.

Be Happy!

Day 15

Refuse to settle for second best

Four hundred years before Jesus, the work that God wanted to do was financed by his people, the Jews. They paid a kind of income tax to the religious leaders who organized society. It was a tenth of their wealth – one in every ten sheep if they were shepherds; every tenth sheaf if they were arable farmers. They called it a tithe.

Tithes freed up certain people so that they didn't have to farm in order to eat – people like priests, worship leaders and the artisans who made the religious life of the

> 'Return to me, and I will return to you,' says the Lord Almighty. 'But you ask, "How are we to return?" Will a mere mortal rob God? Yet you rob me. But you ask, "How do we rob you?" In tithes and offerings. You are under a curse – the whole nation of you – because you are robbing me. Bring the whole tithe into the storehouse, that there may be food in my house. Test me in this,' says the Lord Almighty, 'and see if I will not throw open the floodgates of heaven and pour out so much blessing that you will not have room enough for it.'
>
> *Malachi 3.7–10*

community possible. It also paid for the administration, justice and sanitation systems that kept society functioning. And most importantly, it funded the social security system, which meant that vulnerable people, such as widows, orphaned children and refugees seeking shelter in the community, were not left to die unaided because they couldn't feed themselves. That's a lot for your 10 per cent!

So the Jews made their promises to God and handed over their produce: 'Lord, everything I have comes from you, so this tenth that I give you is already yours. Take it and use it so that everyone in the community can share in the blessings which you have given to me.' Some of it would be burnt as an act of worship simply to please God. Some of it would be put in store so that the religious life of the community could continue. And every three years the whole lot was given away in relief projects for needy people. And the 'rule books' of the Old Testament make it clear that farmers shouldn't pick out the shabbiest tenth, because what was given became holy – set apart and dedicated to God. So only the finest would do! The first tenth. The best tenth.

> Whatever you do, work at it with all your heart, as working for the Lord, not for human masters, since you know that you will receive an inheritance from the Lord as a reward. It is the Lord Christ you are serving.
>
> *Colossians 3.23–24*

Brilliant!

But . . . There's always a but!

But if you are an ancient Jewish farmer, what do you do in a difficult year? For instance, what do you do when two consecutive harvests fail? Are you tempted to think, 'Actually, a half tithe is more appropriate this year because we have only had half the rain.' And if the rains failed for a third time, what then?

A prophet named Malachi could hear heads of households muttering, 'The temple will have to look after itself this year; I need to feed my family.'

> My utmost for his highest.
>
> *Oswald Chambers, Scottish clergyman and teacher, 1874–1917*

'Enough is enough,' wrote Malachi. 'This is robbing God.'

We all make resolutions from time to time, and then find convincing reasons to persuade ourselves that we are justified in weakening. On New Year's Eve I worked out a great end to each day that would bring discipline to a lot of things – exercise, relaxation, reflection. I decided that, at the very end of each day, I would go for a run – down the hill, round through the alley, up by the flyover. Then I'd pour a bath, sit in it reading my Bible as I thought about the day, then flop into bed. The trouble is that none of those are things I really enjoy doing. Jogging is a pain, I'm impatient waiting for the bath to run, and my mind wanders all over the shop when I read the Bible.

So I started letting myself off this routine in limited circumstances. I decided that I would do it every day unless for some reason I wasn't feeling entirely well.

That was fine, but then work became a bit complicated; so I stuck to the resolution unless I wasn't feeling particularly well . . . or I'd had a bad day at the office.

> Do all the good you can,
> by all the means you can,
> in all the ways you can,
> in all the places you can,
> at all the times you can,
> to all the people you can,
> as long as ever you can.
>
> *John Wesley, founder of the Methodist denomination, 1703–91*

That lasted for a while, but I wasn't enjoying it a great deal more. Last week I decided that I would go through my routine every night unless I'm not feeling well, or I've had a bad day at the office . . . or it's dark.

A HAPPY ATTITUDE

I've lost count of the number of promises I have made to God too. 'I will spend time in Bible study every day. I will worship him every Sunday morning. I will give a percentage of what I earn to his work.' But I have lean years, just like the Jewish farmers did. We all do! What happens to our promises in hard times? Do you find yourself saying, 'I will study the Bible, but if I oversleep and have to rush I'll let myself off; I will worship, but if I'm at a party until the early hours of Sunday morning I probably need the sleep more; I will give money, but maybe I should count the percentage after I've paid my tax, not before'?

> Lord God, I have had enough of doing what I can get away with. You deserve more of me, and the world needs more of me. Raise my sights!
> Amen.

Twenty-five centuries after Malachi, we too occasionally need somebody to say, 'Enough is enough!'

Paul pointed out in a letter that is included in what we now know as the New Testament that if we imagined that everything we do was being done for Jesus, it would never occur to us that second best was a reasonable option. Working, giving, exercising, helping in a time of need – everything would be done 'with all your heart'.

I guess that's true. I spent this morning resenting the fact that I didn't get my usual Saturday lie-in because I helped a friend of a friend move house when he couldn't afford a removal firm. To be honest, there hasn't been much satisfaction in it for me because I offered two hours and it took four. I spent the last two hours grumbling that I should be at my desk writing this chapter. Oh, the irony! However, I know for a fact that if it had been Jesus' sofa that battered my shins on every step of the staircase I would be showing off the bruises as if they were purple jewels.

Will approaching life with such a level of commitment to

84

do the best we can bring us happiness? Well, there are no guarantees. But when Malachi tells his Jewish contemporaries to stop begrudging the Lord the best portion of what their work has produced, he ascribes marvellously kind and generous words to God: 'Test me in this. See if I will not throw open the floodgates of heaven and pour out so much blessing that you will not have room enough for it.'

That is God's gracious offer – try it and see what happens! Try offering hours when you would rather be watching television to call on someone who would otherwise sit unvisited in a residential home. Turn time into joy! Try making a gift to a charity that serves the world's poor so that a mother will be re-united with her toddler in a health clinic where she was terrified that he would die from some trivial illness. Turn money into joy! Try committing effort to helping someone whose home or garden has got out of control so that they can get a measure of order back in their lives. Turn sweat into joy! And see what happens.

> **Be happy!**
> Become a blood donor. It is more than giving away a proportion of your money; it's giving away a proportion of your very self. And someone else will live because of it, which is a reason to rejoice.

People are going to be glad to be alive because you make a decision not to settle for second best. And right at this moment they don't even know it yet. Don't you get a kick out of that? Let the floodgates of blessing open, as Malachi wanted. Let's see who gets wet!

Be Happy!

Day 16

Take a stand

Tony Blair once said to me . . .

(You have no idea how much I have wanted to start a chapter with those words! I am now going to ruin it by adding that he said it to 800 others at the same time.)

Tony Blair, former UK Prime Minister, told this story. In 1999 he hosted a meeting of the G8 (the leaders of the world's eight wealthiest nations) in Birmingham. Outside the building were thousands of men and women who had gathered to make known their passionate care for the world's poorest people by persuading governments to cancel the unpayable debts of poor countries. One of the other

> Where there is no revelation, the people cast off restraint; but blessed are those who keep the law. Servants cannot be corrected by mere words; though they understand, they will not respond . . . Pride brings people low, but the lowly in spirit gain honour. The accomplices of thieves are their own enemies; they are put under oath and dare not testify. To fear anyone will prove to be a snare, but whoever trusts in the Lord is kept safe. Many seek an audience with a ruler, but it is from the Lord that one gets justice.
>
> Proverbs 29.18–19, 23–26

national leaders, shocked by the size of the crowd, said to him, 'Have you seen what's going on outside the building?'

'Do you mean the demonstrators?' asked Tony Blair.

And the reply was, 'It's worse than demonstrators; it's Christians!'

I was chuckling about this story today, because I'm really thrilled whenever Christians allow the words they sing on a Sunday to rearrange their priorities from Monday to Saturday. That is when faith counts! In personal terms it changes the things to which we devote time and effort in our everyday lives. In global terms it creates a desire to change the structures of the kingdoms of the world so that they take on the qualities of the kingdom of God.

The campaigning and giving of Christians, alongside others who seek justice, mean that in Uganda there is free primary education for the first time ever. In Bolivia there are new doctors' surgeries so that babies don't die of trivial diseases. In Mozambique roads are being repaired so that business can take place without laboriously having to negotiate potholes big enough to swallow up a man. That's where Christian faith should be – out of the churches and in the potholes. That's what happens when people of faith take a stand.

Not many of us are in positions to change the laws that govern the world. Although I may be wrong, I suspect that you are not someone who creates the rules of our society,

> Put on the full armour of God, so that when the day of evil comes, you may be able to stand your ground, and after you have done everything, to stand. Stand firm then, with the belt of truth buckled around your waist, with the breastplate of righteousness in place, and with your feet fitted with the readiness that comes from the gospel of peace.
>
> *Ephesians 6.13–15*

but you are profoundly affected by them. Like me, you probably wonder when you should accept the standards that have become normal as part of the world's progress, and when you should draw attention to yourself by insisting that there is a better way. In our humdrum, workaday lives, we need to think about when to take a stand to show that we are not seeking to please ourselves, but to please someone altogether more significant.

> A religion of Sunday mass, but of unjust weeks, does not please the Lord. A religion of much praying, but with hypocrisy in the heart, is not Christian. A church that sets itself up only to be well off, to have a lot of money and comfort, but that forgets to protest injustices, would not be the true church of our divine Redeemer.
>
> Oscar Romero, Archbishop of El Salvador, murdered while preaching, 1917–80

It is on occasions like this that the book of Proverbs can make me happy. Proverbs teaches us how faith in God changes what we do in everyday, mundane life. It can show how faith in God has an impact on issues that were not even dreamt of by a human mind when the Bible was written down – genetic modification, television, global warming. But it also advises on issues that are age-old – explicitly mentioned in the book, but with a new expression in this generation, such as the use of drugs, pornography, gambling.

Here are a few that have helped me think about what it means to take a stand for God. The first feature of a person with integrity is that he or she is not swayed by peer pressure into letting God down. As the writer of those time-honoured proverbs put it: 'To fear anyone will prove to be a snare, but whoever trusts in the Lord is kept safe.' If you are trying to decide on the right thing to do, you will weaken if you ask, 'Whatever will people think of me?' Strength lies in asking, 'How can I make God rejoice?' If you are ever called on to be a whistle-blower at work, drawing attention to an injustice, this will be precisely the dilemma that you find yourself in. Proverbs can help you there. But more routinely, it can also help you when you are dubious about whether you should accompany friends to the places they go for entertainment.

Another feature is the ability to restrain yourself from breaking the law, even if everyone else seems to be getting away with it. 'Where there is no revelation, the people cast off restraint; but blessed are those who keep the law.' That is a tough demand if the law concerns the age at which you can see a film, how fully you complete the terms of a business contract, or using your mobile phone while you drive down Croydon High Street. (And yes, if it was you who recklessly overtook me in the silver Audi on the way back from my friend Paul's at midnight last Friday, you were indeed the inspiration for that example.)

> To those who rule and lead us on the earth you, sovereign Master, have given their authority. Lord, make their counsels conform to what is good and pleasing to you, that using reverently, peacefully and gently the power you have given them, they may find favour with you.
>
> *Pope Clement, fourth Bishop of Rome, about 30–99*

> Lord God, I want to take a stand on issues that please you, but I don't want to put my foot in it. Lead me and embolden me, I pray. Amen.

Another way to stand out in a crowd is by attempting to influence people with your example, not just by your words. 'Servants cannot be corrected by mere words; though they understand, they will not respond.' I fully admit that when the Bible talks about masters and servants it sounds irrelevant to this generation. But the joy of reading Proverbs is to find the principle behind the ancient words and readdress it across the centuries. How does this apply to the example you set to your children, your work colleagues, members of your sports team?

And finally, the way to take a stand is with humility, not belligerence. 'Pride brings people low, but the lowly in spirit gain honour.' This is one of the ways that a Christian can have a distinctive approach to standing up for what is right. Even when you are campaigning to influence the most powerful people in the land, it is 'from the Lord that one gets justice'. But what does it mean to be lowly in spirit when the conversation turns insulting to foreigners? Or when someone less talented gets promoted instead of you? What does it mean to be a Christian when a referee fails to notice that your feet were kicked from under you ten centimetres from the penalty area? These are the moments at which seeking the justice of Jesus requires you to do so with the character of Jesus.

> **Be happy!**
> Make your personal contribution to seeking justice throughout the world by writing a letter about an issue of concern to Christians. Send it to the Prime Minister at 10 Downing Street, London, SW1A 2AA, or to the President of the USA at The White House, 1600 Pennsylvania Avenue NW, Washington, DC 20500, USA.

This chapter has taken a meandering route. When I started writing, I thought it was going to be about politicians creating economic policy, but it took a detour via potholes in Mozambique and ended up with some punk aiming for your ankles instead of the football. Taking a stand on behalf of the God of justice might involve any one of those, because you are a follower of Jesus wherever you are during the week, whether it is in Downing Street, on an African dirt track, or slithering around the pitch on a damp Saturday afternoon. You can take a stand sitting in parliament, or you can take a stand lying flat on your face in the sludge. You are worse than a demonstrator; you're a Christian!

Be Happy!

Day 17

Choose wisely

In the days when Jesus' first friends made up their minds to follow him, there was a clear choice to be made. They were choosing between good and evil. They followed him because, in an age of poverty and occupation by an enemy army, they had found someone who rose above that to give them hope, worth and healing. They loved it! But they also had a leader who would occasionally smack them between the eyes by teaching them things that were so challenging that they seemed unattainable.

> [Jesus said,] 'Enter through the narrow gate. For wide is the gate and broad is the road that leads to destruction, and many enter through it. But small is the gate and narrow the road that leads to life, and only a few find it.'
>
> Matthew 7.13–14

People gave up on following Jesus. We sometimes forget that. It took courage and determination to stick with him to the end, and it still does.

Why? Because although the way of Jesus is one in which true happiness is possible, it is not an effortless option. Jesus' ambition was and is to create a society in which everything that is good prospers until we have a world in which people are no longer needy, sad or hurting. And that takes effort by all of us who are his followers. We have choices to make. And some of them are choices we would rather not make.

Unlike Jesus' original followers, the choices we are asked to make are not usually between good and evil. To be honest, most of us don't need more teaching about that – we know that murder is evil and it is not a temptation that we wrestle with daily. I think there's a fair chance that I will get through my whole life without murdering anyone! The same goes for armed robbery, or high treason. I just don't have that kind of life.

> How much better to get wisdom than gold, to choose understanding rather than silver!
> The highway of the upright avoids evil; those who guard their ways guard their lives.
>
> *Proverbs 16.16–17*

Jesus' teaching is about a much more subtle choice. It was reading J. K. Rowling's *Harry Potter* books that helped me grasp this. Dumbledore is the headmaster of Hogwart's Academy and he is the adolescent Harry Potter's mentor. At one point he turns solemnly to Harry and says, 'There are dark days ahead, Harry, days when we will be forced to choose between what is right and what is easy.'

When I read that I realized that it is precisely the predicament of my Christian life here in Croydon. I may not be asked to choose between good and evil very often.

> Let us strive to enter by the narrow gate. Just as the trees cannot bear fruit unless they have stood before the winter storms, so it is with us. This present age is a storm, and it is only through many trials and temptations that we can obtain an inheritance in the Kingdom of Heaven.
>
> *Theodora, Egyptian desert mother (reclusive nun), about 350–400*

That is the inestimable privilege of living in this place at this time. But I have to choose between what is right and what is easy day after day after day.

Examples? When it comes to travel, we all know that hopping in a car is easy. Walking is slow, cycling is hard work, and public transport is minging. But unnecessary journeys on cars and planes are creating havoc with the climate for which our grandchildren are going to pay a mighty price. So what is a Christian going to do – what's right or what's easy?

When it comes to shopping, we all know that buying fairly traded bananas is right. Children on plantations protected by fair trade get an education; children on unprotected plantations die of trivial diseases. But fairly traded bananas cost more (quite a lot more), and the cost of doing what's right mounts up. So what is a Christian going to do – what's right or what's easy?

In relationships, we all know that keeping intimacy unique for one person for a whole lifetime is completely at odds with the standards by which our culture lives. We know in our hearts that society's quality of life is unravelling because faithfulness no longer underpins the way humans regard each other sexually. But it's really tough on an individual when his head is telling him he's a human while his hormones are telling him he's a rabbit. So what is a Christian going to do – what's right or what's easy?

> Better, though difficult,
> the right way to go,
> Than wrong, though easy,
> where the end is woe.
>
> John Bunyan, writer and minister, imprisoned for his faith, 1628–88

I could go on and on. Pay the amount of tax you should, or pay the least tax you can get away with? Write an essay with laborious research, or cut and paste a good one from the internet? Break off with a girlfriend by text message, or endure that horrendous, tearful conversation about why it's time to bring the relationship to an end? Face people who are lonely, vulnerable and utterly draining with friendship or with excuses? What's easy? What's right? What's what?

I think it's time to remind ourselves of what Jesus said. He painted a picture of the small gate and narrow road of what is right, and the wide gate and broad road of what is easy. As we make our way through daily life, choosing between one and the other is the way we mark ourselves out as Jesus' followers. It's ridiculously challenging, isn't it? To number yourself among the few, not among the many. Constantly to ally yourself with what's right, not what's easy. Anything else, Jesus declared, will lead to destruction.

> Lord Jesus, at the hastiest moment of choice, at the toughest moment of temptation, at the best moment of opportunity, don't let me fail you.
> Amen.

Thirty years ago I might have written about how typical it was of Jesus to exaggerate so memorably. But right now, with the environment of our planet in a precarious state, I'm not so sure he was exaggerating at all. Jesus wasn't just saying, 'I want to save your soul.' I believe he was saying, 'I want to save your world.'

Twelve centuries before Jesus, the people of God found themselves on the verge of crossing a river into the land that they believed had been promised to them from ancient times. They were without the inspirational leader, Moses, who had brought them from oppression to independence. Their new leader, Joshua, hadn't really displayed his mettle yet. And the Jordan river was wide and deep. But they were being urged onward, challenged not to take the easy way round but to plunge straight through. They had one heck of a choice to make as they stood on the riverbank, knowing that the Promised Land was on the other side. And they chose to go through. Right through the impossible heart of it. Right through the life-threatening, spirit-sapping mud of it.

Sometimes this is the way God calls his people to go. He doesn't do it with no reason, and he doesn't do it because he wants Christians to be unhappy. Instead he does it because it is the only way that fulfilment and life can follow. The writer of the Proverbs talked of the decisions that need to be made between immediately appealing financial rewards and the long-term benefits that are the choice of those who are wise. 'Choose understanding rather than silver!' he said. 'Those who guard their ways guard their lives.' Happiness follows on from making good choices in the context of meaningful faith and positive attitudes.

Some years later, Joshua brought the volatile people of God face to face with a decision they needed to make – compromising with the habits of the rest of the world, or choosing the best. He said, 'If serving the Lord seems undesirable to you, then choose for yourselves this day whom you will serve, whether the gods your forefathers served beyond the river, or the gods of the Amorites, in whose land you are living. But as for me and my household, we will serve the Lord.' The choice he made is good enough for me!

> **Be happy!**
> Think about the developments in technology that have taken place since you were born. Depending on how old you are they might include the world wide web, mobile phones, credit cards, fast food, even air travel. What are the personal moral questions they pose that previous generations did not have to deal with? If they have encouraged you to do what is easy, rather than what is right, consider what kind of change is in order.

Be Happy!

Day 18

Understand anger

For reasons that I do not understand, I don't get angry very often. When a man pushed rudely past a queue of Londoners and forced his way on to an underground train during this morning's rush hour, people were cursing and shaking their fists. I just laughed. Why's that?

It isn't the case, either, that I am angry deep down, but stifle it. I can see how unhelpful that would be in the long term. Truth to tell, it is not in my nature to be riled by grievances in the way others are. There are exceptions, of course. (And yes, I am thinking of you, the well-heeled and pinch-pocketed lady who harangued me after a sermon because I suggested that it is good to spend extra in order to buy bananas that are fairly traded. And in answer to your question, no, I do not agree that *all* African leaders are idle and corrupt.

> My dear brothers and sisters, take note of this: Everyone should be quick to listen, slow to speak and slow to become angry, for human anger does not bring about the righteous life that God desires.
>
> James 1.19–20

And I wanted to add: Have you ever looked to see in which continent the bananas you buy are grown, Dimwit?)

Sorry! Where was I?

> [Jesus] went into the synagogue, and a man with a shrivelled hand was there. Some of them were looking for a reason to accuse Jesus, so they watched him closely to see if he would heal him on the Sabbath. Jesus said to the man with the shrivelled hand, 'Stand up in front of everyone.' Then Jesus asked them, 'Which is lawful on the Sabbath: to do good or to do evil, to save life or to kill?' But they remained silent. He looked around at them in anger and, deeply distressed at their stubborn hearts, said to the man, 'Stretch out your hand.' He stretched it out, and his hand was completely restored.
>
> *Mark 3.1–5*

In contrast, my best friend Paul has all his anger exploding out of him. As a teenager he moved into the guest room of my house because other places where he had tried to make a home had not worked out. I had been living by myself for sixteen years, so sharing a house with anyone would have taken some getting used to, but sharing it with a firework display was a spectacular shock. There were holes kicked in doors and bellows of midnight rage. Then, after I had wrung my way through an anguished night, Paul would arrive at breakfast full of cheerful affection saying how well he had slept!

It is possible that I have learnt more from Paul than from any other individual. And the most important thing I learnt from him is that nobody does things without a reason. It may not be a good reason, but there is almost always a reason why a person acts in a certain way. Finding and understanding the reason makes other people's actions easier to cope with. That doesn't mean it excuses them, or makes it right that they should go unchallenged, but it does allow the destructive fury to drain out of a situation so that it can be dealt with properly.

I know why Paul was angry during those years – the explanations snake their way back through his childhood, as they do for all of us. I suspect the man on the underground had a reason for behaving so badly (the look on his face told me that he wasn't being obnoxious for a trivial reason).

> What is a healthy Christian approach to anger? Anger is a message, a revelation. Looking at it and understanding the conflict we experience is a key step in illuminating the situation we find ourselves in. If we are attempting to hear God's word, we must listen to anger as carefully as we listen to joy, peace, fear and fatigue.
>
> Kathleen Fischer, North American writer, born 1958

And I know why I was livid with the banana woman, because after leading a church service I am emotionally vulnerable and the smallest criticism feels like being lacerated by a rabid dog.

Anger is in the world for a good reason. Imagine the injustices that would ruin life if every damaging action was accepted with a shrug of the shoulders. To find happiness while being able to survive anger depends on discovering a positive way to express it. And, equally, to receive it. When anger is expressed through violence, through vicious words, or even through glowering silence, misery follows. It is true for both parties, no matter who feels righteous and who feels wronged.

Consider the possibility that the person with whom you are angry might not be the best person to express it to. At least, not in the first place. Talking your anger over with a friend can help you think through the reasons, and put you in a better position to explain your feelings calmly. But explaining your feelings is nevertheless crucial, because bottled-up anger can leak into other areas of your life and spoil them. A friend's advice can help you recognize the right moment to challenge someone, because it is when you are tired or at a point of stress that anger is most likely to become explosive.

The wise men who wrote the proverbs that are recorded in the Old Testament had three pieces of advice about anger. The first was, manage it: 'Fools give full vent to their anger, but the wise keep themselves under control.' The second was, pacify it: 'A gentle answer turns away wrath, but a harsh word stirs up anger.' And the third was, prevent it, because it is utterly predictable that no good will come of it: 'As churning the milk produces butter, and as twisting the nose produces blood, so stirring up anger produces strife.' Three thousand years ago, the people of God were being given precisely the same practical advice as you are in this chapter . . . and with better jokes!

> However just your words, you spoil everything when you speak them with anger.
>
> *John Chrysostom, Bishop of Constantinople, 347–407*

The letter that James wrote, which twenty centuries later we are still able to read in the New Testament, warned Christians what they should do when they felt their tempers rising. He told them to press a mental pause button so that they have a chance to decide whether an outburst is worth it ('be quick to listen'). He told them to find a mechanism that allows them to take control (drink a cup of tea, go for a swim, walk the dog, or whatever it takes to 'be slow to speak'). And he told them to speak coolly, without exaggerating, and without threats ('be slow to become angry').

> Lord God, be the punctuation that makes me pause before destructive phrases come tumbling out. Amen.

Jesus is a fine example to us of how to deal with the anger that we all experience. I suspect (and this is only a guess) that he had the same kind of fiery temperament that is part of young Paul's personality. But he knew precisely the right way to use it to achieve good ends. Standing with his followers outside a village whose inhabitants had grossly insulted him, Jesus listened to the infuriated disciples planning to call down fire from heaven and destroy them. In startling contrast, he told them to calm down, and kept walking. But in the temple at Jerusalem, profoundly angered by the practices that were oppressing the poorest people and keeping them at a distance from their God, Jesus picked his moment to kick tables over and yell. It had precisely the impact he hoped for. And today the way of Jesus may well involve his followers in responding with anger to the great injustices of the world. Using anger on behalf of those who are suffering, in a controlled and focused way, can have an impact on our personal lives. It can give us a proper perspective on what is truly important, and give us the courage to change things. Change ourselves too!

> **Be happy!**
> Make a list, mental or written, of situations that make you angry. And another of people who are angry with you. In each case, try to complete the sentence, 'The reason for this anger is ...' Investigate whether understanding the reasons can help you work out the best way to deal with the problem. Then, calmly, take action.

Guess who I spoke to, full of frustration, after I had been verbally attacked by the woman on the church steps! It was Paul. And would you like to know what he advised me? It was to sit down, eat a banana, and say a prayer. It was probably the tastiest banana I have ever eaten. And it was probably the most heartfelt prayer.

Such brilliant advice! Thank you, mate!

Be Happy!

Day 19

Aim high

In praise of socks! Socks are instantly gratifying. They are simple, comfortable and the colour tells people something about you. The design has never been bettered. They are easy to buy – you don't even have to try them on before you leave the shop. Immediately, cold feet can be warm. To all those relations who, not knowing what else to buy me for birthdays, bought me socks, thank you. You did the right thing!

> I have learned to be content whatever the circumstances. I know what it is to be in need, and I know what it is to have plenty. I have learned the secret of being content in any and every situation, whether well fed or hungry, whether living in plenty or in want. I can do everything through him who gives me strength.
>
> *Philippians 4.11–13*

On the other hand, shoes! (There is something wrong with that sentence. I'll work it out in a minute.) Shoes can be a bit of a handful. (Nope! Still can't decide! Press on!) In the shop, you have to try them on for size in front of a stranger who wants your money. For the first few days they make you walk with a limp because the leather is so unforgiving. You grimace your way through a series of blisters on the very day when you want to look smartest. And just when you have broken them in and they begin to feel comfortable, they get scuffed on a treacherous kerb and no amount of polishing will ever make them perfect again.

However, if someone told you that, for an afternoon stroll across the park, you could only wear one or the other, you wouldn't have a moment's hesitation over which to choose. Durable worth wins out over instant pleasure every time.

> [Jesus said,] Provide purses for yourselves that will not wear out, a treasure in heaven that will not be exhausted, where no thief comes near and no moth destroys. For where your treasure is, there your heart will be also.'
>
> Luke 12.33–34

We are coming close to the halfway point of this spiritual journey, and this is the first time I have stopped to ask myself what happiness *isn't*!

It isn't a passing enjoyment. A happy person is not someone whose life has had so many occasions when they enjoyed themselves that their sum total has exceeded a pass mark and given them an exam qualification. Advertisers use the word in this sense, but it is deceptive. My local pub advertises a 'happy hour' from five o'clock to six thirty in the evening, when alcoholic drinks are half price, but I can't think of any reason why that was the appropriate title. I suppose 'cheap ninety minutes' didn't sound enticing.

I don't believe either that happiness is merely good fortune. This is true despite the fact that the word *happ* arrived in the English language because the Vikings brought it with them when they invaded England nine centuries ago. For them, the word meant good luck. We don't use it much now (although we still speak of an unlucky accident as a mishap). When happy people find themselves faced with misfortune, they don't curse their fate, but find ways of handling or changing the circumstances.

The influence of your genes, your parents and events during your earliest years can, of course, have a profound impact on how readily you can settle into a happy life. A start in life that involved unkindness does not condemn you to a life of unhappiness. The events through which you lived cannot be changed. However, your outlook on life and your resolve to adopt particular attitudes is yours to choose. If rejection or cruelty featured in your formative years it may be that outside help is needed in order for you to create a new worldview for yourself. That help can improve your health and it is available – get it!

> We hold these truths to be self-evident, that all men are created equal, that they are endowed by their Creator with certain unalienable rights, that among these are life, liberty and the pursuit of happiness.
>
> *The American Declaration of Independence, developed from a draft by Thomas Jefferson, third President of the USA, 1743–1826*

There seem to be three dimensions of happiness about which the Bible talks. The first is a level of basic content. It can give a basic appreciation that life is pleasant, and is found when essential needs are adequately met – enough food, a safe place to live, companionship, and enjoyment of a beautiful view, a funny film or an emotional piece of music. These are the simple socks of life, and I thank God for them. When the writer of one of the psalms praised God for 'wine that gladdens human hearts, oil to make their faces shine, and bread that sustains their hearts', he was thanking God for a very real experience of happiness.

However, there is a happiness that is beyond this, and to which Paul referred when he told the Christians in Philippi that he had learnt how to be content even if he had to do without those things. He wrote, 'I know what it is to be in need, and I know what it is to have plenty. I have learned the secret of being content in any and every situation.' And the secret was that he had discovered that the strength God gave him was not dependent on being in luxury or in difficulty. You too can find that buoyancy if you reach a point at which you know your own unique virtues and strengths well enough to allow them to enhance your life. The happiness that comes from this is like the shoes of life because it takes experience, both good and bad, to break it in. Like Paul, discovering that you are a person who has the strength to cope with both plenty and need gives you a very secure footing when you are striding through the rain.

> The heart is rich when it is content, and it is always content when its desires are fixed on God. Nothing can bring greater happiness than doing God's will for the love of God.
>
> *Migel Febres Cordero-Munzo, Ecuadorean monk and academic, 1854–1910*

But even beyond that is a level of happiness for which I can't think of a comparison with a type of footwear. It comes when you are so comfortable with the virtues and values that God has created within you that you no longer think about how to use them for your own happiness, but work out how they serve a purpose greater than your own self. This is the way of Jesus, and it fills your life with meaning. It must be what he was thinking of when he talked about 'purses that will not wear out'. His belief was that the things you acquire and achieve in this way create 'treasure in heaven' – treasure that is aglow with generosity, shared by many and has an impact that will reverberate through eternity.

> O God the hope of the world, understand my pain, be part of my pleasure, and point me towards the very best. Amen.

I can't think of a better example for these three dimensions of happiness than sex. In its own right it makes a person happy – God has made it that way to give life moments of delight. It gives a fundamental happiness which, even after years of practice, never lasts quite long enough before it becomes a pleasant memory.

However, when sex is part of deep commitment, loyalty and enduring love, it takes on a different quality altogether. This is the happiness of lasting, personal fulfilment. It is the context that the Bible suggests is proper for sex – not because Christian teaching seeks to deny the value of feeling wonderful during sex, but because God wants people to get more and deeper richness from it.

And then, when sex becomes the cause of a new human life entering the world, a different kind of happiness altogether can become part of human experience – the happiness that overflows with meaning. When, in the goodness of God, a birth is planned and welcomed, it ushers in wonder, hope and generosity that sees far beyond the present. The investment of care that is involved in nurturing a new life into independence points towards eternity.

> **Be happy!**
> Spend some time making a list of things that give you pleasure – it doesn't matter whether they are as basic as fresh air or as complex as the contents of your iPod. Thank God for them. But then go on to think about how each of them could play its part in a richer way in giving fulfilment to your life as an individual, and meaningful service to a cause greater than your personal success.

Pleasant happiness; fulfilling happiness; meaningful happiness. Each requires a greater investment than the one before, but the quality of life that comes with them repays the effort many times over. And all of them comprehensively surpass the transitory excitement that is meant to lure you and me into a bar that has a happy hour. They are not based on consumption, but on attitude. And attitude always was and always will be a matter of choice.

So there you have it! Passing pleasure is socks and enduring happiness is shoes.

And cheap alcohol is pants!

A happy body

Be Happy!
Day 20
Recognize your dignity

Here's something that got me thinking! Why did John baptize his cousin Jesus? Why not the other way round, which would have made more sense? Even John the Baptist protested at first that it was all wrong. Christians believe that Jesus was without sin of any kind. He of all people did not need to seek forgiveness, let alone be baptized as a sign of that. Why did the only person who didn't need to be baptized deliberately decide that was what he should do?

The significance of Jesus' baptism is rooted in another core Christian belief – that, in Jesus, God himself was walking on the earth as a human being. God become totally

Jesus came from Galilee to the Jordan to be baptised by John. But John tried to deter him, saying, 'I need to be baptised by you, and do you come to me?' Jesus replied, 'Let it be so now; it is proper for us to do this to fulfil all righteousness.' Then John consented.
As soon as Jesus was baptised, he went up out of the water. At that moment heaven was opened, and he saw the Spirit of God descending like a dove and lighting on him. And a voice from heaven said, 'This is my Son, whom I love; with him I am well pleased.'

Matthew 3.13–17

111

human! No infinite powers; no absolute knowledge! Instead, God identified with every one of the bruises and weaknesses and needs of human life – including the need to be baptized.

Last Christmas I pushed the boat out a bit and bought my mother what I thought was quite a special present. I gave her a mobile phone. Her face was a treat. She was excited that now she too would be part of the new generation that has instant access to everyone. I phoned up on Boxing Day to find out how she was getting on. There was no reply at all from the mobile phone, so I resorted to the landline. My father picked up the phone, and I asked how she was managing with the charging, and the texting, and the directory, and the messages, and the entering of the phone numbers, and the answerphone, and the reception, and the telephoning, and . . .

I could tell from my father's silence that it wasn't going as smoothly as I had hoped. 'Well,' he said. 'It's a bit of a struggle to understand.'

> That which was from the beginning, which we have heard, which we have seen with our eyes, which we have looked at and our hands have touched – this we proclaim concerning the Word of life. The life appeared; we have seen it and testify to it, and we proclaim to you the eternal life, which was with the Father and has appeared to us . . . his Son, Jesus Christ.
>
> I John 1.1–3

I was slightly frustrated, because I had spent a long time the previous day going through it. 'Pass the phone over to her,' I said, 'I'll give her some more instructions.' I could hear him hesitating. 'It's OK,' I said. 'Just give her the message.'

He went away and came back a moment later. He said, 'Well, she says that to be honest, she doesn't want better instructions or more messages. If she's going to understand the wretched thing, what she really needs is her son to visit in person.'

That is why Jesus came to earth. If we are going to understand how to live and how to be at one with God, he could have sent better instructions and more messages for a million years. But it wouldn't have achieved what was needed. So his Son visited in person.

> Recognize your dignity, O Christian. Once you have been made to share in the divine nature, do not by your evil conduct return to the base servanthood of the past. Keep in mind of whose head and body you are a member.
>
> *Pope Leo I, about 400–61*

A human among humans. God among those who desperately need God.

It's an extraordinary thought! The Creator looks at his own earth, ruined by wrongdoing and failure, and laments, 'What can be done?' But from the depths of time eternal he has always known what has to be done. So he slips on a pair of Levi jeans, he reaches for a Marks and Spencer sweater, he slaps on some aftershave, and he says, 'OK, I'll go!' And there he is, walking along Oxford Street among us.

If it is true that Jesus Christ is God, then he has conferred on the human body more dignity than can possibly be conceived. Because of Jesus, being human is now something full of the most wonderful potential. No wonder Matthew records the voice of God saying, 'This is my Son, whom I love; with him I am well pleased.'

> He became what we are so that he might make us what he is.
>
> *Athanasius, Bishop of Alexandria, 296–373*

Let me tell you some staggering facts about Jesus' body. I hope these facts make you gasp at how stupendous he was. Jesus had eyes that could distinguish one million

113

different colours. His extraordinary heart beat 100,000 times every day of his life. Jesus' blood vessels were so long that together they could have circled the earth twice. He had a skin that never stopped replacing itself until his dying day. Even after 2,000 years, humankind has never encountered a structure as complex as his brain.

How do I know all these things? I know them because every single one of them is true of you as well. God is as pleased with your body as he was with Jesus' body.

Knowing that I was going to type those words, I took a long look at myself in the mirror this morning. To be honest I need a bit of reassurance that this body, certainly past half-time and heading for a goalless draw, still has all the dignity of someone crafted by God. Wrinkles have dug deep. The scars of a rather battered life are going to be there for ever now. And with an irony that no one has ever explained satisfactorily to me, hair has stopped growing on my head and started growing in my ears.

All this has made me ask questions. How is my friend Carla going to react to this chapter when she reads it sitting in a wheelchair? Or Heather, who claims to have read every word I have written, but who has never been able to hear my voice? Can someone who lives with a disfigured body, or one that causes them repeated pain, or one with complex disabilities, sense that their flesh, blood and bone are infused with the dignity of Jesus?

> Lord God, it is an honour that I share with Jesus the cartilage, corpuscles and marrow of life. Help me look at my body, botched and blotched, and be glad that you put me in it. Amen.

Well, first of all I need to thank Carla and Heather for the happy times I have spent with them, and ask them to forgive me if I have got this wrong. But this is what I have been thinking. Next to my mirror I have a reproduction of an utterly magnificent picture painted in 1495 by an Italian artist called Ercole de Roberti (which you can now see free of charge in Liverpool or on the website of the Walker Art Gallery). It shows a middle-aged Mary, dressed in black, heartbroken as she cradles the dead body of her son Jesus in her lap. The Jesus she evidently loves so deeply is blood-drained, scarred, ugly. And yet the overwhelming impact of the scene is of ravishing tenderness. Dignity, in fact! I have spent a long, long time looking at this painting, because for 500 years it has been telling people something profound. Injured bodies, hurting bodies, unsightly bodies – these too share the majesty of having been inhabited by God. These too have had a breathtaking natural dignity conferred on them because Jesus was once like this. These are bodies that deserve to be happy.

> **Be happy!**
> Put some effort into treating your body with the dignity that Jesus has conferred on it. Recognize how wonderful it is by treating it well. Take some exercise or get some fresh air, then relax and breathe deeply. Book a back massage at a health centre. Have a bath and put on some flattering clothes – not to please anyone else, but to enjoy the fact that you have been blessed with a human body, just like the Saviour of the world was.

I can't see your body from where I am sitting right now. (Two problems – short sight and lack of bionic superhero powers.) However, I hope you are happy in your body. You can be, if you choose to be. I hope you feel able to present it looking its best, but without feeling obliged to fight what time is doing to it in the natural logic of things. I hope you feel able to enjoy what you and Jesus have in common, but choose to worship him rather than worship your own looks. And I hope your heart will swell today with the dignity of pumping human blood.

Be Happy!

Day 21

Be kind to your body

OK, you might as well know the truth! It's a Thursday evening. I'm sitting in the National Theatre in London. I am by myself, with an hour to spare before the play begins, so I am having something to eat and writing this chapter by hand on a paper serviette. On my left there is a piece of salmon – pert, pink and perfect – next to a leafy salad and an apple. They will be so good for me! On my right there is a glass of white wine and a slab of cake only slightly smaller than St Paul's Cathedral. I can't pretend that either of those will do me any good at all.

> Who has woe? Who has sorrow? Who has strife? Who has complaints? Who has needless bruises? Who has bloodshot eyes? Those who linger over wine, who go to sample bowls of mixed wine. Do not gaze at wine when it is red, when it sparkles in the cup, when it goes down smoothly! In the end it bites like a snake and poisons like a viper. Your eyes will see strange sights and your mind imagine confusing things. You will be like one sleeping on the high seas, lying on top of the rigging. 'They hit me,' you will say, 'but I'm not hurt! They beat me, but I don't feel it! When will I wake up so I can have another drink?'
>
> *Proverbs 23.29–35*

So that's me! I can't lecture you on how to eat healthily, because I'm not a saint. But on the other hand, I haven't let what I consume spoil my ability to enjoy my life, and I am hoping that this can be true for you as well. I am two jeans sizes bigger than I was as a teenager, and I'm not proud of that. But I have never smoked, so I can kiss someone without them retching. I am a happy medium – in virtue, fitness and trousers.

The fact is that what you eat and drink has an impact on your mood. To eat well is one of the steps towards a happy life. In the Bible the writer of the book of Ecclesiastes was a cynical so-and-so,

> Whether you eat or drink or whatever you do, do it all for the glory of God.
>
> *I Corinthians 10.31*

but even he knew that eating was one of the great pleasures of life: 'Go, eat your food with gladness, and drink your wine with a joyful heart, for it is now that God favours what you do.' But equally, the writers of the Old Testament knew that there was misery to be found in abusing the goodness of food: 'Do not join those who drink too much wine or gorge themselves on meat, for drunkards and gluttons become poor, and drowsiness clothes them in rags.'

> When you begin to talk more slowly, walk more slowly, eat more slowly, then it may be possible that we can begin to do something about your spiritual life.
>
> *Francis de Sales, Bishop of Geneva, 1567–1622*

So, halfway through this forty-day spiritual journey, today is a good moment to ask how something as simple as taking care over what you eat and drink can make you happier. Of course, there is a simple answer to the question as well as a complicated one – once in a while a cream meringue can splatter the bull's-eye like nothing else on earth! However, scientific research has given us all a bit more detail to help us maximize the value of particular foods for a contented life. You become more alert when you eat food that is high in protein, such as fish, poultry, cheese or eggs. Your calmness is enriched by eating carbohydrates, such as wholemeal bread, whole-grain rice, cereals and fruit. Foods that help to protect you against disease include green vegetables, nuts, berries and tea. And although it seems almost too basic to mention, drinking a steady quantity of water all through the day can improve your well-being effortlessly.

The secret to all this seems to be balance. I doubt that stuffing yourself during your holidays and then dieting for a month to compensate is going to make you consistently happy. However, being kind to your body through what you put into it as days and weeks go by seems to be the way to treat yourself with the dignity that God intends for you. So keep an eye on what you eat – both the quantity and the content. Enjoying your food does not mean piling a plate high with it; it means putting tasty things on it, just sufficient, and wasting none.

What constitutes good food? Variety is a fine start! The more different colours you have on your plate the more likely the meal is to be nutritious (unless you are eating a whole bowl of Smarties, which is definitely excessive). Fruit and vegetables are pretty much the healthiest thing you can eat, and we need five little handfuls every day. They are full of fibre and antioxidants. (I haven't the faintest idea what an antioxidant is, but I knew you'd be impressed if I threw that word in.) A banana is my favourite happiness fruit – have you ever seen one that wasn't smiling?

> Food ought to be a refreshment for the body, and not a burden.
>
> *Bonaventure, theologian and philosopher, 1221–74*

Conversely, eating less of certain foods will give you a healthier outlook on life. Products using carbohydrates that have been refined before you eat them fill you up with all the wrong things. So try not to eat white bread or white flour, or to drink products that have got a heap of sugar in them. And cut down on the amount of saturated fats you eat by choosing low-fat dairy products, and grilling food instead of frying it.

Does this mean you can never eat a plate of thick, gorgeous chips again? Don't be stupid! This is not a book about how to be miserable. The trick is to regard foods that are full of fat, salt or sugar as treats, and enjoy them all the more because you only have them occasionally. But if lunch is a packet of crisps and a fizzy drink every single day, it will not lead to the happiness you hope for.

What I am going to say next will make me unpopular with some people too! In the long run, you genuinely will be happier if you stop smoking cigarettes. Yes, yes, I know it's going to be incredibly tough and will fill you with cravings and yuckiness to start with. But you will have more money to spend, you'll live longer, your children won't get ill so often, and you won't get skin that looks like an elephant's bottom. No contest!

> Lord God, help me to enjoy every mouthful I eat and every glassful I drink, without feeling rotten about it afterwards. Amen.

And while we're on the subject of drugs, for goodness sake don't imagine that illegal ones are likely to make you happy in any lasting sense. Ecstasy will make you buzz for a bit; cannabis will make you chill for a bit; LSD will make you weird for a bit. Three cheers! But I am big-headed enough to think that you are reading this book because you want to know my opinion. So here it is – taking them is respectively stupid, stupid and stupid.

And that brings me back to the empty wineglass in front me which, just over an hour ago, had a very nice Chablis in it. I am well aware that some readers will be dismayed that I have been working my way through it while I wrote this chapter, because for the last hundred years (since water became safe to drink in this country) some Christians have abstained from alcohol altogether because it is addictive, dangerous and can ruin relationships.

I have always liked the Bible's approach to alcohol. It regards it as one of the good things that God has given for our happiness, urgently insists that abusing it is going to have extremely bad consequences, and warns us to be careful with it instead of haranguing us. The knockabout extract from Proverbs quoted above is a good example. The Bible writers seem to urge you to seek a balanced and cautious approach to this, as with everything else you consume.

> **Be happy!**
> As days go by, while you read the second half of this book, monitor what you are eating and drinking more closely than usual. Drink a bit more water and a bit less cola. Eat a few more vegetables and not so many ready meals. Enjoy the flavour of a wholemeal sandwich instead of a tasteless white one. Test your body by seeing whether you are any happier after a few weeks in which you guzzle less salt and sugar. And if any issues about drink, food or drugs are making you anxious, resolve to take a trip to your GP before you reach the last page.

And so in this chapter I have tried to take the same approach. I hope that being kind to your body in this way will, over time, make you glad through and through.

Be Happy!
Day 22
Enjoy creation's goodness

This chapter is about how you can find true happiness by thinking about the way the whole godly project of existence began. And it begins with a task! So would you be kind enough to go and fetch a Bible – either from a bookshelf or from a library. I'll wait while you are gone . . .

OK, are you back?

Please open it at the first page. Skip all the small print (which I have to confess I've never read) and find the first chapter of Genesis. The first thing I would like you to do is to look at the Bible. Not the words, but the actual book! Look at the contrasts and patterns. Black ink on white paper. Soft pages against a hard cover. Monochrome text against a coloured wrapper. The straight lines of the columns and the curved letters of the script. Light falling on some parts of the page and shadow on the rest. Just think

> God said, 'Let there be light,' and there was light. God saw that the light was good, and he separated the light from the darkness. God called the light 'day', and the darkness he called 'night'. And there was evening, and there was morning – the first day.
>
> *Genesis 1.3–5*

– this is the glorious variety of the way God has created the world, and you haven't even read any of the words yet!

This array of contrasts in a graceful equilibrium is precisely what you discover when you come to read it. The first chapter of the Bible is all about beauty and balance. It tells the story of how the world came to be in the way the great Hebrew storytellers must have passed it on for hundreds and hundreds of years, sitting around the campfire at night. Imagine children listening, still and open-mouthed, with the firelight flickering on their faces as the awesome greatness of God becomes clear to them for the first time.

> God saw all that he had made, and it was very good. And there was evening, and there was morning – the sixth day. Thus the heavens and the earth were completed in all their vast array.
>
> Genesis 1.31—2.1

At God's bidding, day is separated from night, light is separated from dark, water is separated from land, work is separated from rest. Everything is in equilibrium. First there is light, and later there are suns and stars. Next there is air and water, and later they are full of birds and fish. Subsequently there is land and greenery, and later it is inhabited by animals and humans.

> Glory be to God for dappled things ...
> All things counter, original, spare, strange;
> Whatever is fickle, freckled, (who knows how?),
> With swift, slow; sweet, sour; adazzle, dim,
> He fathers forth whose beauty is past change,
> Praise Him.
>
> Gerard Manley Hopkins, poet, 1844–89

What you are looking at in the first chapter of the Bible is the basis of what we now call ecology. Humans, animals, plants and minerals are in delicate balance – a single community of creation. Each part depending on each other part; every part dependent on God. It is as though the writer of Genesis had a glimmer of insight into something that 3,000 years hence people would study for three years in order to gain a science degree.

Forgive me, I am being fanciful! I shouldn't really pretend that the poet who composed the first book of the Bible had a scientific knowledge ahead of his time. But God did! Alleluia!

So what do we know because of the marvellous chapter that begins the Christian scriptures? We know that we are not here by accident. We are in a world of structure, order and rhythm. And, most important of all, we are in a world of meaning. And that means, you matter. *You* are worth something. The world would be different if you had not been born into it.

> Joy, beautiful spark of God,
> Kiss the world's millions!
> Brothers, beyond the starry canopy
> A loving Father surely dwells.
> Do you recognize the Creator?
> Be happy as a hero at the moment of victory!
>
> Part of the 'Ode to Joy' that concludes Beethoven's Ninth Symphony, Friedrich Schiller, poet, 1759–1805

There is one word that is used more than any other in the story of how God brought the cosmos into being. Can you guess what it is?

It is 'and'. This is disappointing, since it proves nothing!

However, there is another word that comes up again and again, so often that you can't help but notice how crucial it is in the account of the world's creation. If you still have a Bible in front of you, it should be obvious what it is. Good, good, good, good, good, good, good. Let a truth that God wants you to know sink in – the world would be worse if you had not been born into it. (Writing this has made me so cheerful – it's not often you get a chance to say these things!)

What else does the start of the Bible tell us about the six billion years during which our wonderful, blue-green blob has orbited the sun? That the world is not in the hands of impersonal forces controlling humankind (so stuff horoscopes!). That there aren't a thousand little gods bickering over how our world should be (so rejoice in worshipping one God who knows what he is doing). That the material world is not evil in itself (so enjoy your lunch, because it looks good, it smells good, and it will do you good). And, best of all, that there is a plan (so when you sit down and watch the news this evening, do not despair – we are the creation of a God who is planning a good end no matter what a mess humans make of his work).

But it would be reckless to talk about God the Creator without being reminded of the part he has given to human beings in sustaining his creation. It is our responsibility to care for this planet and to preserve the ecology that is described with such splendour. However, the truth is that humans are using the resources of the earth to comfort and enrich this generation without sufficient thought for its implications for the generations of humans yet to come. That cannot possibly be pleasing to God. When we stop the world being a place of happiness for our fellow humans it is, frankly, a sin. But it is also a sin to stop the world being a place of happiness for the humans who will walk the earth in the decades after our time here has expired.

> It's all so beautiful.
> Thank you.
> Amen.

On Friday night I was at the Royal Albert Hall listening to Beethoven's Ninth Symphony, gloriously played and sung. That piece of music is one of the finest statements about the possibility of raw joy in the face of every doubt that life can throw at it. And I found myself thinking that it would be so, so sad for the humans to go the way of the dinosaurs. Beethoven's music is so sublime that I can't bear the thought that there might come a time when there are no people left on earth to appreciate the height of achievement to which humans once rose. I have no doubt whatever that, should it happen, God would not give up. He would get to work to bring something new and good out of the situation. That is, after all, what he has done again and again throughout the centuries. The message of the first chapter of the Bible is that the Composer of Creation moves in the muscle of the world, continually making and remaking. But that is not an excuse to be smug about the fact that we have been fortunate enough to be granted life in an unspeakably beautiful world. Rather it is a wake-up call to remember that as part of one, single community of creation, we cannot take its magnificence for granted.

The moment has come for Christian men and women to take a stand. As the children of God, lead the way in sustaining his earth! In our actions, in our example, in our conversations, in our campaigning, in our recycling, in our prayers, in our evangelism, in holding our hopes high. We are in a world that is good, good, good, good, good, good, good. With that big blessing comes a big responsibility. Let's joyfully renew our commitment to being the stewards of God the Creator.

> ## Be happy!
> Take a look at the rubber seals around the windows of a car. Unless it is absolutely brand new, you will notice that they are beginning to turn green. This is because, even in this most unlikely place, plant life is taking hold. It shows the staggering force of the urge to generate life that God has placed in the universe. How astonishing! Be thrilled! And then decide how you are going to find an alternative to using the car to keep it that way.

Be Happy!

Day 23

Get active

Exercise and sleep! That's what this chapter is about. They are both things that I am happy to make room for in my life, although I like one of them much more than the other.

I love sleep. I can't do without it! I go to enormous lengths to get some every day. I have been known to forsake entire, lengthy expository sermons in my crazed pursuit of it.

But let's talk about the more energetic one first. The fact is that there is a correlation between cheerfulness and fitness. Scientific research has told us the reason for that in recent decades, but people who are tuned into the wisdom of God's world have known it for centuries. The writer of the Bible's Proverbs, ever practical, tied the two together 3,000 years ago: 'A cheerful look brings joy to the heart, and good news gives health to the bones.' And the writers of the New Testament, whom you would expect to have no time for anything but spiritual advice, made it clear that they were concerned for every aspect of the well-being of the followers of Jesus.

> To my dear friend Gaius, whom I love in the truth. Dear friend, I pray that you may enjoy good health and that all may go well with you, even as your soul is getting along well.
>
> 3 John 1–2

At the time when Paul was writing the letters that now form part of the Bible, he was aware that the philosophy of the ancient Greeks was that the body was an evil thing, and that the beauty of the human soul was trapped inside its sordid flesh. But God had revealed the truth to be different altogether. The human body was something full of goodness (Paul compared it to a temple), so looking after it was important. As a mentor to a young man called Timothy, full of potential as a Christian leader, he recommended that exercise was good, while spiritual fitness was even better. He put it like this: 'Train yourself to be godly. For physical training is of some value, but godliness has value for all things, holding promise for both the present life and the life to come.'

> Many are asking, 'Who can show us any good?'
> Let the light of your face shine upon us, O Lord.
> You have filled my heart with greater joy
> than when their grain and new wine abound.
> I will lie down and sleep in peace, for you alone, O Lord, make me dwell in safety.
>
> *Psalm 4.6–8*

The problem with recommending exercise is that it makes me sound like the ghastly PE teacher I had in my secondary school, who still makes appearances in my dreams thirty years later. (It is the hairy arms that loom largest in my memory. Did everyone's PE teacher have arms as hairy as mine did? Were the male ones like that as well?) I wish I had known then what I know now – that exercise makes you happy. The feel-good element that comes after energetic activity is not imaginary; there is a reason for it. Blood and oxygen swoop round the body prompting your pituitary gland to release compounds called endorphins, and this makes you feel contented both physically and mentally.

127

A HAPPY BODY

The fact that exercise makes you happy is more significant for me than the other well-rehearsed benefits. We have been told a million times that if we keep active it will control our weight, make us less prone to illness, keep pain at bay, and increase our prospect of a long life. To be honest, though, those sound like nagging. But to discover that exercise makes you enjoy life more is compelling.

> Examine thy customs of diet, sleep, exercise, apparel and the like, and try in anything thou shalt judge hurtful, to discontinue it little by little. If thou dost find any inconvenience by the change, come back to it again, for it is hard to distinguish that which is generally held good and wholesome from that which is good particularly and fit for thine own body.
>
> *Francis Bacon, philosopher, 1561–1626*

The secret is to find something that you *want* to do. It's not meant to be a punishment! For competitive people, sport is the ideal way to combine pleasure with fitness, but there are many ways to be physically active if you simply don't care whether you win or lose. And they need not be expensive. Before you pay a huge amount to join a gym that you stop attending after the first month, think about whether your starting point could be taking a dog for a regular walk or learning to dance. They will never be Olympic sports, but they are a step in the right direction.

If company is likely to help you stick at it, join a group that is exercising regularly. But some people prefer the fact that exercise gives them an opportunity to be by themselves, thinking while they run, swim, walk or jiggle on

> Holy, holy, holy – and that means hale and hearty and whole and healthy with a mind set heavenwards.
>
> *Eric Gill, sculptor, 1882–1940*

a machine. The choice is yours to make. Build up your level of activity slowly and take advice (including advice from a doctor if you haven't been active for a long time). To aim for three periods per week when you are lively for half an hour is a good ambition, but anything is better than nothing.

One of the advantages of being active is that people who exercise regularly tend to be able to fall asleep more quickly, sleep more deeply, and wake up feeling refreshed. Most people need seven or eight hours' sleep every night, although a few people get away with five and others need nine. The Bible is very practical about sleep. There are places where it is critical of those who are still in bed when they should be up and energetic. But there are other places where the Bible firmly advocates rest. The fact is that a balanced life, with work, leisure and rest (using all those terms in a loose sense) is one that is most likely to bring content. If you work to earn a living, take all the holidays to which you are entitled, and turn off the machines that allow people to email you wherever you happen to be. Don't apologize for doing so! You will be a better worker for it.

> Lord God, give me the resolve to change my flabby standards, my unfit attitudes, and my unfulfilled intentions. I don't expect to be a champion; I'd just be happy not to be an also-ran. Amen.

In this world of beautiful rhythm in which God has placed us, night follows day, sleep follows waking, rest follows activity. This is his design for living, and fighting it over a long period is merely wrestling his plan.

If you struggle to sleep, try every natural means to get the most out of it before you resort to medication. There are several things that you can do to help. One is to slow down during the final part of the day by doing whatever you find relaxing – perhaps reading, listening to the radio, taking a bath. Marking the close of the day with prayer, thinking through the events of the past hours with quiet thanksgiving, is not only good for the spirit, but good for the body. If you are able to get into a routine that involves doing this at the same time every day, your brain will get used to the fact that it is time to sleep.

Other practical advice is that a firm mattress is better than a soft one, and that you will fall asleep more readily if your fingers and toes are warm. Coffee last thing at night will keep you awake, and alcohol may send you to sleep quickly but is more likely to leave you awake and fidgety in the middle of the night. And it is worth spending a little money to make sure that you have a pillow that supports you properly (firm if you sleep on your side; softer if you sleep on your back). You will spend a third of your life cuddled up to it, so a good pillow is not an extravagance.

Throughout all this we are in the care of a God who never sleeps. He rests (which is one of the first things the Bible tells us about him) but he never sleeps. Knowing that allowed the writer of one of the psalms to surrender himself joyfully into the care of the Lord night after night after night. He wrote: 'I will lie down and sleep in peace, for you alone, O Lord, make me dwell in safety.' I plan to say those very words as I get into bed in . . . hmm . . . about ten minutes' time.

> **Be happy!**
> Think about some ways in which you could be more active without substantially disrupting your life. For instance, use the stairs on occasions when you have been taking the lift, leave the car behind and walk to nearby destinations, stop work in the middle of the day and get out into the fresh air (even if it is only to post a letter or buy a sandwich). Reward yourself by buying a new pillow that fully supports your head and neck, and enjoy sleeping better.

Be Happy!

Day 24

Manage stress

Three things that I have seen happen during recent years! A man uncontrollably stressed by a telephone call slams down the receiver, rips the wire clean out of the wall, and throws the phone through the open window. A woman bursts into tears and runs from the room when asked, quite innocently, 'Who is your line manager?' A clergyman, his mind completely distracted by emotional pressures, stops after a few words of a communion prayer because he realizes that there is no bread and wine in front of him and that he is leading the wrong service.

> [Jesus said,] 'Come to me, all you who are weary and burdened, and I will give you rest. Take my yoke upon you and learn from me, for I am gentle and humble in heart, and you will find rest for your souls. For my yoke is easy and my burden is light.'
>
> *Matthew 11.28–30*

Stress does unpredictable things to you. I chose those examples because they are quirky. For the most part, stress does not reveal itself in dramatic moments like that – it just builds invisibly until you feel that you simply cannot cope. In some ways the examples I chose were positive incidents, because they were signs to everyone that the person needed help, and thus turning points at which issues could be addressed. In the examples I didn't choose, stress gnawed unseen inside people until their body protested by becoming ill, or their work deteriorated so badly that they needed to leave it temporarily or permanently.

Stress is going to be complicated to write about, because although everyone knows when they are feeling it, it is not easy to define. Pressure is a good feeling for most of us because it gets things done. But there comes a moment when pressure becomes so great that it feels like something we have no way of controlling. That is when it escalates into the kind of stress that can make a person deeply unhappy.

Jesus clearly understood what it meant to live with stress. This in itself is a surprise, because we tend to assume that if we had lived in a different century the pace of life would have been slower and the pressures fewer. But Jesus' heart went out to 'weary and burdened' people.

An even greater surprise is the fact that he suggested the main cause of stress in people's lives was placed on them by their religion. Every rabbi or religious leader of his day had his own pattern of behaviour that his followers would adopt in order to be true adherents to the Jewish law. It was called a rabbi's 'yoke' (after the wooden bar used in ploughing to make sure the ox goes the right direction). Jesus knew that men and women wanted to show devotion to God, but that the demands put on them by other rabbis

> Humble yourselves, therefore, under God's mighty hand, that he may lift you up in due time. Cast all your anxiety on him because he cares for you. Be self-controlled and alert ... And the God of all grace, who called you to his eternal glory in Christ, after you have suffered a little while, will himself restore you and make you strong, firm and steadfast.
>
> I Peter 5.6–10

Come now, turn aside for a while from your daily employment, escape for a moment from the tumult of your thoughts. Put aside your weighty cares, let your burdensome distractions wait, free yourself for God and rest awhile in him. Enter the inner chamber of your soul, shut out everything except God and that which can help you in seeking him, and when you have shut the door, seek him. Now, my soul, say to God, 'I seek your face Lord; it is your face that I seek.'

Anselm, Archbishop of Canterbury, 1033–1109

were burdensome. People were weighed down with rules that were restrictive and expensive, and threatened with God's displeasure if they failed. However, Jesus' 'yoke' was completely different. He was not threatening, as others had been; he was gentle and humble. Jesus' pattern was easy to follow and the burden of it was light. All that was required was to turn to Jesus, believing the good news he proclaimed, and God would take people to himself.

The truth of Jesus' teaching is still a profound help in stressful times, 2,000 years on. No matter what other difficulties may be adding to your stress, Jesus is one to whom you can come in confidence that he requires nothing oppressive from you. Religious leaders might be a slightly different matter – Jesus' followers can still sometimes be demanding! But that's different. Forgive them for being human, and take your anxieties straight to Jesus. That is where you will find rest.

> Pressure can change you into something quite precious, quite wonderful, quite beautiful and extremely hard.
>
> *Maya Angelou, poet, born 1928*

So what practical help can coming to Jesus be in times of stress? First, Jesus knows what you are dealing with, and so in his presence you too can identify what the problem is. Very often we know what the symptoms are – tension, sleeplessness, undefined anger, fretfulness – but cannot be specific about what it would take to put it right. Prayerful reflection can identify the precise causes, rather than the general misery, which is a big help when it comes to managing them.

Managing stress requires a clear head with which to make decisions, and that too is something with which Jesus can help because when we come to him we are coming to the God who is bigger than the problem. The decision may be to face the problem that is causing you stress head on (which might be unpleasant, especially if it involves dealing with a relationship that is causing pain at home or at work). But there are other possible decisions – changing your own approach in the hope that it will provoke a reciprocal change, sidestepping the issue so that it no longer impacts directly on you, or seeking more time to deal with it so that you can climb the ladder out of the trench one step at a time. Tell yourself repeatedly, 'It is for times just like these that I am a Christian. I am not dealing with this alone.'

> Lord Jesus, here are the anxieties I have been carrying about events in my life. Please take them. I don't want them back. Amen.

May I tell you what brings me most stress? It is not turbulent emotions or a heavy workload, both of which I seem programmed to cope with. It is machines on which I totally depend failing, when I am helpless to know how to mend or even understand them. The main offenders are the computer, the car and the central heating. And right now, right this very second, the broken washing machine over which I have come very close to shedding tears this morning!

Yes, I know that's pathetic! But my stress is not the same as your stress. I will try to understand why you can't cope with things that seem unproblematic to me if you return the favour. I know that these are the parts of my life over which I am extremely vulnerable, and I have strategies for getting through life that minimize the stress, which I hope might be helpful to you.

Planning ahead is an obvious one. If you know that a task is going to take a week to fulfil, begin it seven days before it's due, not the evening before. This may involve being very protective of your time and saying no to things that will distract you from an important task. And get on with stuff – fretting about things saps energy that you could be putting into solving problems.

Clear the clutter that trips you up. I mean this both literally (tidying clothes, throwing away rubbish, doing the washing up) and mentally (making lists of what needs to be done, and knowing where to get help – such as the phone number of the plumber – grrr!).

And finally, make space in your life for the things that will help put stress into a context of content – friends, laughter, relaxation, sex, exercise, fun, prayer. At some point in your life one of these will be the very thing that is causing the stress, so you need to have

Be happy!

Write down three things in your life at present that involve no stress at all – they could be particular places, friendships, hobbies or activities. Even if they are relatively small things, such as a favourite food or an uplifting piece of music, make a note. While you are doing so, you will be tempted to have the pleasure they give you diminished by other thoughts about stressful situations. Swat those aside! Instead concentrate on the fact that there is a sight, a sound, a flavour or a scent that is problem-free. Repeatedly and gratefully go there (either for real or in your imagination) knowing that Jesus accompanies you.

given generous space to as many of them as are appropriate so that the others can keep you buoyant at that time.

Jesus' life was planned, uncluttered, and rich with enjoyment. That is where the strategy comes from, and that is why he can be someone who brings rest. Trust him!

And now, if you will excuse me, I have some shirts that need to be hand-washed.

Be Happy!

Day 25

Break a bad cycle

I don't know how to walk. I only realized this recently. I learnt how to do it at such an early age that I can't remember how it happened. I suppose I must have been coaxed to put one leg forward and then the other, wobbled, fell, and kept on trying until I got the hang of balancing on my tiny feet. But I don't do all that now – I just get up and stride. In fact, if I thought about what I was doing I would probably make a hash of it.

> I have the desire to do what is good, but I cannot carry it out. For what I do is not the good I want to do; no, the evil I do not want to do – this I keep on doing ...What a wretched man I am! Who will rescue me from this body of death? Thanks be to God – through Jesus Christ our Lord.
>
> Romans 7.18, 19, 25

Truth to tell, I don't know how to drive either – I just sit in the car and do it. When Paul was a teenager I tried to give him lessons, but by that stage I had been driving for twenty years and no longer thought about the mechanics of it. I remembered the bit about looking in the mirror before you pull away from the kerb, but I forgot the bit about putting the clutch down between gears. It was too obvious to mention. Big crunch!

That's what habit does for you! It ingrains behaviour so deeply that you give no thought to it. Of course, there are both good and bad habits. Many of my good habits have been there since I was a child. For instance, I always eat everything that's on my plate, and I can still hear my mother's voice insisting on it. She has shaped the part of me that hates waste.

But with damaging habits, the first steps in addressing them are to recognize what they are, acknowledge that they diminish your happiness, and stop blaming other people for them. They might be things that you do but would find very difficult to stop because your body has become so accustomed to them. It takes a surprisingly short time for you to grow so used to nicotine, caffeine or alcohol that you feel uncomfortable without them. In fact, sugar and salt have the same impact, and carry the added danger that you don't get disapproving glances when you consume them.

> It is for freedom that Christ has set us free. Stand firm, then, and do not let yourselves be burdened again by a yoke of slavery.
>
> *Galatians 5.1*

Some cycles of behaviour are secret, of course. The internet has made it much easier to return again and again to unhealthy activities that no one else knows you are doing – gambling, talking nonsense to strangers, or linking endlessly from website to website when you are too tired to go to bed.

> There are two freedoms – the false, where a man is free to do what he likes; the true, where a man is free to do what he ought.
>
> *Charles Kingsley, clergyman and novelist, 1819–75*

Other habits are more difficult to put a name to, even though they damage you just as much. Losing your temper is one that everyone around you notices. Or swearing or driving aggressively. Some are more subtle – being pessimistic, undermining people, having a low opinion of yourself. None of these things are necessarily part of the real you. If you are able to identify them as habits that you have got into, then with determination you can get out of them as well.

Temptation is a ferociously strong impulse. I have a vivid memory of being in a newsagent, aged thirteen, hormones zapping and temptation zinging. The shopkeeper came across to where I was standing looking up at the magazines on the top shelf. 'Are you trying to look at the porn?' he asked accusingly.

'Definitely not,' I retorted categorically. And it was a completely honest answer. The truth is that I was trying *not* to look at the porn.

So how can God help you break cycles of behaviour with which you have become comfortable even though you know deep within you that they are holding you back? You have to want him to. Genuinely – because he won't be fooled if you tell him one thing while you are thinking another! Try to work out the reason why you have got into a particular habit. What is it that is missing from your life that you are replacing with behaviour that is not doing you any good? For instance, looking at pornography is a way of making up in your imagination for something unfulfilled about the place sex has in your real life. Is there a more godly way of dealing with that than such an easy, sleazy habit?

> Every saint has a past and every sinner has a future.
>
> Oscar Wilde, playwright, 1854–1900

Seeing a habit through God's eyes can also help you weigh up its results. Human nature is fiendishly clever when it comes to breaking the link between our actions and their consequences. Even though we know beyond dispute that consuming certain things means that we are likely to die younger and face old age with miserable health, we persuade ourselves that we will be the exception, or that medicine will have advanced to provide a cure for the damage we are doing. In the Bible, Paul sighed, 'I have the desire to do what is good, but I cannot carry it out.' It's a familiar lament! He looked to Jesus as the saviour who could break the cycle. He went on: 'Who will rescue me from this body of death? Thanks be to God – through Jesus Christ our Lord.'

In the middle of the twentieth century, the very same truth was at the heart of the programme devised by Alcoholics Anonymous to help people overcome addictive behaviour. Their programme for breaking bad cycles grew from an explicitly Christian foundation, but even now its secular restatement asks people to recognize that they do not have by themselves the ability to control compulsion, but 'a Power greater than yourself' could restore you. Name that Power as you seek to break a habit. Call him Jesus!

> Lord God, the only thing I want to keep coming back to is you. Amen.

Devise a strategy for changing your behaviour. Have a definite motive so that your mind is focused on why you want a different future. Get the support you need, either from an established group (secular or Christian, depending on where you feel comfortable), or by confiding in a friend who wants the best for you. When temptation lurches into your mind, swat it away like a fly that has no business pooing on your picnic. When temptation comes close in a tangible way, walk away from it so that you don't have it assaulting your eyes, nose and ears. Practise saying no over and over again – it will become less difficult as time goes by. And celebrate small successes – give yourself a healthy treat when you manage to get through a set length of time without the unhealthy habit.

And pray! God is willing you to succeed in this, and every time you pray you will be reminded that he is on your side.

When I was very young my grandparents lived in a North London house that was heated by coal fires. I used to think that the fireplace in the living room was magnificent, and the most splendid part was a large brass knob whose function was to pull out the grate, using a pair of tongs. The reflection of the flames, dancing around it in a golden circle, was mesmerizing to me. My grandparents told me again and again that I must never touch the knob – only *they* were allowed to handle it! But the dazzle and glow was a huge temptation. I couldn't imagine why my grandparents were so selfish that they kept for themselves the wonderful pleasure that would obviously follow from touching it. And so, on one occasion when they had momentarily slipped out of the room, I crawled close, moved the fireguard and grabbed hold of the knob.

I don't think I need to tell you the rest of the story, because you can guess how unpleasant it is. However, I do need to tell you that I have learnt a great deal about temptation from it. Habits are hard to break because their easy pleasure is alluring. Be strong! You are cared for by a good God. He can change what you can't – and it will end in happiness.

> ### Be happy!
> Break a habit! If the behaviour you want to change is related to the internet, use a search engine to find accountability software – a free service that delivers a report of the websites you have visited to two trusted friends. If it is related to your health, join a group in which you will find others who are trying to break cycles of damaging behaviour and give each other encouragement. If it is a pattern of destructive emotions, find someone supportive to talk to about it. The end of this forty-day journey is two weeks away – a good initial target.

Be Happy!

Day 26

Seize opportunities

Yesterday it snowed. Not just a sleety sprinkle, but a cascade. In this part of the country we have not experienced snow like it for nearly twenty years. It was a day off, so I woke up later than usual and lay in bed listening to the noises outside my flat. I knew something unusual had happened overnight, because I could hear no vehicles, and the voices had a cushioned hush. And then I peeked behind the curtain into the white, eccentric light.

> God's voice thunders in marvellous ways;
> he does great things beyond our understanding.
> He says to the snow, 'Fall on the earth,'
> and to the rain shower, 'Be a mighty downpour.'
> So that everyone he has made may know his work,
> he stops all mortals from their labour.
>
> Job 37.5–7

I was fumbling to get my wellingtons on with toast in one hand and my phone in the other. I scrunched down the hill towards my friends through a Christmas cake of anticipation. Croydon looked utterly beautiful (words that I doubt will ever be written again by a human being during my lifetime)!

Then this morning I looked at the newspaper and

could barely believe the headline. It was: 'Parents in fury over school snow closures'. I was stunned. But as I spoke to my neighbours, I realized that the headline was entirely accurate. For half of them, the most significant element of the day had been the aggravation caused by having to rethink their working day. The other half were bemoaning the inconvenience of not being able to travel.

> There is a time for everything, and a season for every activity under heaven:
> a time to be born and a time to die,
> a time to plant and a time to uproot,
> a time to kill and a time to heal,
> a time to tear down and a time to build,
> a time to weep and a time to laugh,
> a time to mourn and a time to dance.
>
> *Ecclesiastes 3.1–4*

The Inuit have eighteen different words for snow. Big deal! Croydon residents have eighteen different words for being bad-tempered (grumpy, irritable, testy, cantankerous, peevish, crabby, cranky, disgruntled, sullen, surly, cross, truculent, crotchety, grouchy, petulant, sulky, irascible and waspish).

Now, I do not have children of my own. (Do I wish I had? Profoundly and earnestly. Has that reduced my life to unhappiness? No!) I fully admit that I may have misunderstood the point of parenthood. And I certainly have no concept of how very difficult it must be for a single parent who has a low-paid job from which she would be sacked if she did not battle her desperate way through a whiteout. However, when I picture what my life would have been like with children, what comes to mind is that, if we were really blessed, amid all the tantrums, diarrhoea, exhaustion, frightening trips to casualty and humiliations on parents' day, one morning, one glorious morning during

> Oh what does grief matter! What does misfortune matter, if one knows how to be happy? Do you know, I cannot understand how anyone can pass by a green tree, and not feel happy only to look at it! How anyone can talk to a man and not feel happy in loving him! Oh, it is my own fault that I cannot express myself well enough. But there are lovely things at every step I take, things which even the most miserable man must recognize as beautiful. Look at a little child! Look at God's day-dawn! Look at the grass growing! Look at the eyes that love you, as they gaze back into your eyes!
>
> *From* The Idiot, *by Fyodor Dostoevsky, Russian novelist, 1821–81*

their infancy, snow would tumble from the heavens, and we would go out and build a snowman.

Events happen that bring the expectations of your life to a standstill. Very often they are associated with death. Even the most work-obsessed or rigorously organized people cease what they are doing when a bereavement strikes. For a few days, children stop going to school. Appointments get cancelled. Mourning takes over because, in the face of the great non-negotiable realities of God's world, the other stuff simply doesn't matter.

Society does not collapse. Organizations and employers manage. That is what death can teach us. But isn't it sad that it takes something as appalling as a bereavement to allow us to learn this. Occasionally glorious and beautiful things can disrupt our lives as well, and they need to be grasped. An unexpected success or an emotional surprise

> To struggle, laugh and smile in the midst of aggression; to be cheerful, to hope, to love and not to be intimidated – this is the grace of God.
>
> *Arnaldo Zenteno, Nicaraguan theologian, born 1948*

for which the only appropriate response is to abandon all plans and rejoice. Or a white wonderland!

Seize opportunities! And get a sense of perspective even if it means that twenty emails go unanswered or a child delays learning about quadratic equations for a day. Or perhaps a week. Or maybe for ever. Seize opportunities, and thank God with all your being that you are enjoying their spontaneous, disruptive glory on a day when you haven't had to telephone the undertaker.

Fifty years before Jesus, the Roman poet Horace wrote, 'While we're talking, envious time is flying. *Carpe diem!* Seize the day!' Two thousand years later, the pace of life has accelerated rapidly, but we still need to learn the lesson. We still need to capture the specialness of the present moment, knowing that it will never come again. Stop wishing you were somewhere else or someone different, and take advantage of what is possible because you are living this life, in this place, at this very second. As Paul wrote to the Christians in Ephesus, 'Be very careful how you live – not as unwise but as wise, making the most of every opportunity.'

> Lord God of all eternity, show me what there is to be happy about in my life right at this very moment. I don't want to wait for heaven before I find out what happiness is, because at this rate I'll be dead before I get there.
> Amen.

If you are single, opportunities present themselves that could never have occurred if you were in a romantic relationship. Enjoy them without exhausting yourself in envy of your married friends. And if you are married, don't let the joy of it drain away because you resent the freedoms you have lost.

I was best man at a friend's wedding. He stayed at my flat overnight after the stag party so that we could go down to the church together. In the morning I took a cup of tea to him in the bathroom. 'Hey, it's just occurred to me,' he laughed. 'This is my last shower as a virgin.' That tickled me, so after the service and reception, when the dancing had reached its height, I told his new wife what he had said. She looked at the sweat dripping down his shirt, puckered her nose at the unmistakeable smell of vigorous dancing in a small room, and said: 'That was *not* your last shower as a virgin!'

To be single, to be married, to be a parent, to be childless – all are bursting with the potential for happiness. They all bring challenges too, and none of them keeps sadness at bay for ever. And of course, all those states can come to an end – sometimes with celebration; sometimes with tears. But to be happy in the present moment comes from focusing on what they offer you, not what they deny you. There is, after all, a time for every activity under heaven. For every activity that God has given us on this magnificent, unpredictable planet!

On the London underground last month a young woman was weeping uncontrollably. Paralysed with embarrassment, nobody knew what to do. We all glanced at her occasionally and then looked back at our newspapers, knowing that we would be getting off within a couple of minutes, and persuading ourselves that there

> ### Be happy!
> Do something ridiculous and spontaneous that will increase the amount of happiness in your world. Something that could only happen right this moment! If the sun is shining, go for a picnic. If it is raining, dance in it. If there is someone in the room with a sense of humour, tickle them. If someone lives alone next door, buy them flowers. And if you are reading in bed, go to sleep with a smile on your face in anticipation of the brilliant dreams you are about to enjoy.

was nothing worthwhile we could do to improve matters. Then, as we rolled into a station, the man opposite me got up. He reached inside his briefcase and pulled out a bunch of flowers that clearly had been destined for someone else. He gave them to her, said gently, 'It can't be as bad as all that,' and left the train.

I wish I'd done that! I wish I had summoned the spontaneity to do that. But instead, I learnt from it. Next time something similar happens, I will seize the opportunity.

Speaking of which, please excuse me if I stop writing now. I need to go and retrieve a scarf, a hat and a carrot that are currently sinking towards the ground in a Croydon park. There is, after all, a time for everything!

A happy spirit

Be Happy!
Day 27
Seek Jesus

In the middle of my fifth decade Jesus reached out and grabbed hold of me. This seems a strange thing for a man to write, particularly one who has been going to church ever since he was pushed there in a pram.

A colleague was quizzing me about why I identify myself as a Christian. 'Is it because you enjoy church services?' (Erm . . . not really! Sometimes they're a bit boring.) 'Is it because you think our society is wicked?' (Actually, no!

> Looking at his disciples, [Jesus] said:
> 'Blessed are you who are poor,
> for yours is the kingdom of God.
> Blessed are you who hunger now,
> for you will be satisfied.
> Blessed are you who weep now,
> for you will laugh.
> Blessed are you when people hate you,
> when they exclude you and insult you . . .
> rejoice in that day and leap for joy,
> because great is your reward in heaven . . .
> But woe to you who are rich,
> for you have already received your comfort.'
>
> *Luke 6.20–24*

In fact I am very positive about our culture as a tolerant, civilized democracy.) 'Is it because you hate gays and Muslims?' (Saints preserve us, no! And it breaks my heart that our churches appear so lamentably loveless that you need to ask me that question.) 'So why?'

Providing a response took me back to reading again the story of Jesus in the Gospel of Luke. The answer to the question of why I am a Christian is provided by the life and teaching of the person whom I esteem more highly than anyone else in human history. I need someone to ask me about him now and again, because I keep forgetting why I admire Jesus so very much. I never forget, obviously, that he is the Saviour

> You know the grace of our Lord Jesus Christ, that though he was rich, yet for your sakes he became poor, so that you through his poverty might become rich.
>
> *2 Corinthians 8.9*

of humankind. But that trips off my tongue so easily that sometimes I say it without any real meaning.

The way people talk about Jesus often makes him seem saintly, worthy, slightly bland. But he clearly was not like that to the fishermen who risked their livelihoods to follow him. He evidently didn't seem like that to the devoted women who gave their money to pay for his ministry. And as for the children who naturally made themselves at home in his company, well, they obviously found him wonderful, because children don't hang around being polite when they're bored. All these people found him to be the one I rediscovered as I read his biography – Jesus, the technicolour, compelling, consoling, inviting, creative, unexpected, delightful, thundering, revolutionary, glorious mountain of a man! Who just so happens also to be the almighty God!

May I tell you the thought that occupied my mind as I reread Luke's Gospel? It was this: what would I make of Jesus if I didn't know how the story ended? If I were a contemporary of his and had no idea that the cross and the resurrection lay ahead, what would I think of him then? If I were one of his original followers, why Jesus?

First, because in a world where such unfair things take place, he had the courage to stand against injustice. Then, as now, rich people were able to create systems that kept themselves comfortable at the expense of poor people. In AD 30 the businessmen of the Roman empire had control of the fishing industry. Based in Jerusalem, they were buying fish in bulk, salting them (which gave them a much longer shelf life than fresh fish), and exporting them through the empire. Consumers who lived miles from the sea were able to enjoy eating sardines as a luxury for the first time. Because the businesses had grown so huge, they called the shots, and the people who came off worst were the fishermen who worked by the coast, getting a lower and lower price in the market place. It was so unfair. No wonder Peter, James and John left their fishing nets behind when they heard that Jesus was offering an alternative. Can you imagine a politician today saying: 'Woe to you rich for you have taken advantage of the poor and have already received your comfort'? No, neither can I!

> Jesus came when everything was growing old. He made it all new.
>
> Augustine, Bishop of Hippo in North Africa, 354–430

> Thirst for Jesus, so that you will stagger drunk with his love for you.
>
> Abraham of Nethpra, monk and writer in what is now Iraq, about 600–50

But more than that, Jesus had the ability to do something about it. 'Blessed are you who hunger now, for you will be satisfied.' We are used to hearing empty promises, but this was not an empty promise. Jesus' first hearers believed that they would genuinely be satisfied and find hope.

They believed Jesus' assertion that poor people are better off than rich people because they grasped two things. The first was that we have a spiritual standing that is not related in any way to our physical conditions, and can transcend them. Who has the blessing of God? Is it those who earn it? I'm afraid not. Those who are closest to the kingdom of God are those who are most helpless. That was Jesus' message.

Come like a child; it's the only way! Come uneducated, inexperienced, helpless, vulnerable, penniless, confused, weak, crying. God will do everything you need to bring you to him. Why are the poor blessed? Because they are the closest to the helplessness that is the only way God can do anything for us. The qualifications will get in the way, the house will get in the way, the promotion will get in the way, the money will get in the way. If you want to know the blessing of God you need to get yourself in a position to say: 'These things mean nothing to me; the Lord Jesus is everything.' It's tough for those who are rich, for they have already received their comfort. Not impossible, but tough! But, 'Blessed are those who are poor, for theirs is the kingdom of God.'

> Lord Jesus, let me be honest! I want your blessing, but I don't want to be poor. I want to be filled by you, but I don't want to go hungry. I want to rejoice to know you, but I don't want to be hated for it. Have mercy, my friend and Lord. Take me as I am, I pray, and make of me what you want me to be. Amen.

The second realization of Jesus' followers was that we have an eternal destiny that will exceed our present circumstances in every conceivable way. 'Rejoice in that day,' said Jesus, 'And leap for joy, for great is your reward in heaven.' We have a God of compassion and, in the goodness of his plan, heaven will compensate those who have suffered because of the greed of their fellow humans. 'Blessed are you who weep now, for you will laugh.' That is the destiny of those whose lives have been blighted by violence, by hunger, by hate.

And that stupendous compassion of Jesus for those with whom he wanted to spend eternity is another reason why he has seized my imagination like no other human. Just think about whose company he sought out – the outsiders, the lonely, the sick, those who felt that society had given up on them. He stayed single, defied convention, kept on the move, adored the company of his friends, needed times to be alone. I am absolutely convinced that he would have found a place in his entourage for me!

Why Jesus? Because of his justice and because of his compassion. For me that's why! Because he speaks to the heart of what is wrong in the world, and tells us what needs to be done to put it right. The way of compassion is a challenging way. It won't be easy. It will involve me having a little less so that others can have a little. But that is how the world will be healed.

> Be happy!
> If you find the life and teaching of Jesus compelling, find places to record that fact. In a diary, on a blog, beneath your signature, or as part of a profile, write: 'Follower of Jesus Christ'.

About the same time that Jesus grabbed hold of me, Facebook was founded and grabbed hold of the rest of the world. I signed up, of course. One of the boxes that you are required to fill in to create your profile asks for your religious views. I typed in 'Follower of Jesus Christ'. I did so with pride flowing out of my fingertips. I am persuaded that, no matter what happens to me, to the church or to the world, that is not going to change.

Be Happy!
Day 28
Let God take control

Imagine you are a glove. (This is going to be a bit weird. Sorry! Just trust me!)

Imagine you are a glove. You are lying on a shelf in a shop alongside your glovey friends, and you are yearning for a better life. In fact, a better world! Surely the glove world could be improved by better fabrics – away with wool, give us leather! Surely the best thing to happen would be brighter colours, or shinier buttons, or sexier stitching. Mittens would be better, or rebranding yourselves as gauntlets. Or perhaps the best thing would be to change the shelf you are on to one that offers a better view of the sky.

Well, congratulations to you in the glove fraternity for having the determination to improve your lot. As far as it

> [The apostles asked Jesus], 'Lord, are you at this time going to restore the kingdom to Israel?' He said to them: 'It is not for you to know the times or dates the Father has set by his own authority. But you will receive power when the Holy Spirit comes on you; and you will be my witnesses in Jerusalem, and in all Judea and Samaria, and to the ends of the earth.' After he said this, he was taken up before their very eyes, and a cloud hid him from their sight.
>
> Acts 1.6–9

goes, all those things would make life better. You've got as far as your glove-bound imagination can take you, and that's fine.

Then, unexpectedly one day, someone comes into the shop and purchases one of your number. She puts it on, easing her fingers into the extremities. What an astonishing revelation! All the improvements that you previously thought would be so good pale to insignificance. They were just outward changes. Suddenly you realize what a glove is for. Transformed from the inside, you discover that your world can be changed utterly. It actually made no difference whether you were leather or wool, mitten or gauntlet, top shelf or bottom. Now you are inhabited, you realize that the reason you are in the world is to carry an umbrella, or do the washing up, or plant roses, or conduct a life-saving operation. You can't be blamed for having had such small ambitions when you were on the shelf – it was all you knew. But with a hand inside you, you can achieve things previously unimaginable.

> On the evening of that first day of the week, when the disciples were together, with the doors locked for fear of the Jews, Jesus came and stood among them and said, 'Peace be with you!' After he said this, he showed them his hands and side. The disciples were overjoyed when they saw the Lord. Again Jesus said, 'Peace be with you! As the Father has sent me, I am sending you.' And with that he breathed on them and said, 'Receive the Holy Spirit.'
>
> *John 20.19–22*

That's what was happening to the first followers of Jesus during the days when they realized that they were never going to see him again. They were wrestling with the fact that Jesus had gone just at the moment when they thought their world was going to improve. In the Acts of the Apostles, the book that's named after them, you can see them struggling as best they could to make things better.

'Please can we have Jesus back alive with us?' No, you can't. That was a special, glorious time in your lives. It won't continue.

'In that case, is this the moment for the political revolution we have been longing for, in which the oppressive Roman rulers are overthrown?' No, you can't have that. The timing of that is in God's gift, not yours.

'Then please can we at least see a vision of Jesus to inspire us?' Not any more, sadly. At least, not until one day in the future when Jesus brings the created order to its climax on the Day of Justice.

'So is there nothing whatever we can do to make our world better?' Wait! Wait!

> Abbot Lot came to Abbot Joseph and said, 'Father, as best I can I keep my little fast and my little rule, my prayer, meditation and contemplative silence. I strive to cleanse my heart of yearning for things I do not need. Is there anything else I should do?' His teacher rose in reply and stretched out his hands to heaven. His fingers became like ten torches. He said, 'Why not be totally changed into fire?'
>
> Lot, Egyptian desert father, about 350–400

Be patient! You are right that there is nothing *you* can do. But God has something in mind that is way beyond your imagination. Go back to Jerusalem and get ready to be staggered by what is to come!

And, thank goodness, they did! Thank goodness, because ours would be a very different world if they hadn't. If they had got Jesus back, he would have lived another thirty years and died of old age. If there had been a political coup, Barabbas would have become governor of Judaea and ruled by thuggery. If they had been granted visions of Jesus, they would have faded bit by bit as the last apostles went to their graves. I don't know where that would have left us, but you certainly wouldn't be reading this book today.

What actually happened was as far beyond their imagination as a hand is beyond a glove's imagination. It wasn't their outside that changed, but their inside. The Holy Spirit came. Staggering! No longer were they staring at the sky. Every last finger of them was engaged on a plan that would change the world. It was a plan for Jerusalem (yes), but it was

> Jesus didn't promise to change the circumstances around us, but he did promise great peace and pure joy to those who would learn to believe that God actually controls all things.
>
> *Merlin Carothers, North American army chaplain, born 1923*

also a plan for Judaea (yes), and a plan for Samaria (oh my goodness, yes), and a plan for the ends of the earth (stone me, I had no idea)!

The plan, though, was not going to be fulfilled by a miraculous display of God's might. Instead, it was going to be fulfilled by witnesses. That's you and me, incidentally. 'You will be my witnesses,' said Jesus, 'in Croydon, and in all Britain and Europe, and to the ends of the earth.' (I may have copied that slightly wrong, but I have an optician's appointment shortly. I'm sure it's the gist of what the Bible says.)

> Holy Spirit of God, less of me and more of you, I pray.
> Amen.

Enlivened by the Holy Spirit I can do what none of the disciples, and not even Jesus, could have done – talk to a stranger I fell into conversation with on one of the Croydon trams last Wednesday. So can you! And you can chat about how being conscious of God has made you happier. And with any luck, as you get off, he'll say (as he did to me), 'You're the first Christian I've met who isn't all "thou shalt not".' And secretly you'll yelp, 'Goal! Kingdom of God one; darkness and despair nil.'

Because the apostles let God take control, he was able to direct them towards a gospel of peace, not a declaration of war. It could have been different; it could have been calamitous. An uprising might have defeated the Romans – fired up as they were, I reckon those early disciples could have achieved that, or at least died in a glorious cause. However, the work of the Spirit was going to change all subsequent history and establish a kingdom that would last for eternity, and not by force of arms or revolutionary politics.

That too has an impact on how we live and pray today. It is a reminder that the decisive rout of evil is not something that will be achieved through armies, dread or force, but only through a transformation of the human heart. It must be the prayer of every Christian that the peace of our troubled times will be achieved not through having better weapons, but through having a better vision for how to live together in the lands of Jerusalem, Judaea, Samaria and the ends of the earth. And also that the peace of our troubled families and neighbourhoods will be achieved not by raised voices, but by improved reasoning. What might happen if the Holy Spirit could inhabit us so completely that things that surpass our previous thinking can take place?

> **Be happy!**
> Take time to think about your current ambitions – they might concern your job, your children, your education, your relationships, your finance and possessions, even your church. What would make you truly happy in each area? Would you be prepared to open yourself to God taking control, even if it revolutionized your plans?

So choose! Stand there blinking at the sky, wishing things could be put back to how they used to be. Or invite the Holy Spirit to lead you courageously on into new things that you couldn't even picture before, but that are possible if he takes control. New loves, new hopes, new opportunities. Happiness comes when you feel that you and God's plan fit like a hand in a glove.

Be Happy!

Day 29

Pray gladly

I do talk to God *a lot*. I doubt that I talk to God the way one is ideally supposed to, but it does happen very often during the course of a day. It's never first thing in the morning like they told me I should do when I was in Sunday school. (If you ever met me at seven thirty on Croydon station you would realize why I don't presume to engage God in conversation at a point in the day when I have usually only managed to get one eye open.)

> Do not be anxious about anything, but in everything, by prayer and petition, with thanksgiving, present your requests to God.
>
> *Philippians 4.6*

Once I have got myself going, though, I am quite happy to tell God what I am feeling about almost everyone on the planet – individuals and armies; the famous and the forgotten; Amy Winehouse, obviously; the president of Uzbekistan (because he is such a total slimebucket); virtually every British professional sportsperson (because the newspapers keep telling us that they haven't got a prayer); Pascal, who makes my sandwich each day and has made me smile every lunchtime since 2006; squirrels (I'm not quite sure why – I think it's because they have a tail like a question mark and so I have a crisis over the meaning of life every time I see one);

162

teenage boys (I'm not sure why either – I just think that anyone who walks down the street with their pants showing needs someone to pray for them); people with fish signs on the back of their car (because they usually swerve life-threateningly in front of you at the traffic lights); most of the living people I have ever known; most of the dead people I have ever known; and late on Sunday nights, the entire cast of *The Simpsons*, for whom I can't stop myself praying despite the fact that I am well aware they are all fictional.

> I pray that you, being rooted and established in love, may have power, together with all the saints, to grasp how wide and long and high and deep is the love of Christ, and to know this love that surpasses knowledge – that you may be filled to the measure of all the fullness of God. Now to him who is able to do immeasurably more than all we ask or imagine, according to his power that is at work within us, to him be glory in the church and in Christ Jesus throughout all generations, for ever and ever! Amen.
>
> *Ephesians 3.17–21*

Any one of those has probably disqualified me from having anything sensible to say about prayer. There are plenty of books that will tell you that praying for dead people and animated characters is not the best way to exercise your spirituality. To be honest, though, I don't think that we really need to read another book about prayer; what we actually need is to get on and do it. Make a habit of it! So that every five minutes you are thinking,

> Thieves do not readily attack a place where they see royal weapons prepared against them, and the one who has prayer grafted into his heart is not easily robbed by thieves of the mind.
>
> *Mark the Ascetic, monk and writer, about 400–50*

'Oh, I'll pray about that!' Not making a big deal of it – just involving God in whatever is in your mind. And then repeating that again and again and again.

I can't imagine God reacting by saying, 'That's not the proper way to pray – I think I'll send a lightning bolt.' I reckon God must be delighted when he becomes so infused in our lives that it is the natural thing to have him involved in each moment, as we make every decision, relate to every friend, even pass every stranger. You don't need a new theory of prayer in order to do that; you just need practice.

Back in Sunday school they used to teach us: 'Don't let prayer turn into a shopping list for God.' But the truth is that I do that all the time now. All the time! It's either a long list of things to say sorry for, or a long list of things I'm anxious about. Then there's a long list of things I am thankful for. I keep muttering, 'I love my life,' for one reason or another – and I've got to be grateful to someone, so it's just as well there's a God to hear me. So *of course* I bring God a long list of things I need. It would be daft not to!

Does all this prayer change things in space and time? I honestly don't know. I know it changes me – that's good enough. Does God step in and change the order of the cosmos because I have accidentally bought the wrong train ticket and don't want to be stranded at Birmingham? I doubt it, actually. But it doesn't

> When the dream in our heart is one that God has planted there, a strange happiness flows into us. At that moment all the spiritual resources of the universe are released to help us. Our praying is then at one with the will of God and becomes a channel for the Creator's joyous, triumphant purposes for us and our world.
>
> *Catherine Marshall, North American writer, 1914–83*

seem to stop me praying about these things in the hope that it will change something.

That did happen to me, actually. I found myself changing trains at Birmingham on 4 October with a ticket that clearly said 5 October, even though I know *categorically* that I asked for the right thing. I was heading for the ticket office, praying, 'Oh please God, no. Not Birmingham! It's the only station in the world where it is perpetual night!'

I explained to the man behind the desk what had gone wrong, and asked if he could help me out. To my astonishment, I didn't get a penalty fare; I got a replacement ticket and a smile. That really isn't supposed to happen. Did the fact that I prayed about it change the situation? You'll have to take that up with God. But I walked back on to the train thinking: 'What a brilliant man that was; what a brilliant life I have; what a brilliant God there is!' I am absolutely sure that the change within myself was put there by the Lord.

I was still thinking about it several days and hundreds of prayers later, so you can see why I am so encouraged to pray for anything and everything, good or bad, completely reckless of the rules. I am trusting God to take care of how he responds. And by watching how he responds, I am learning what pleases him. And my life will be richer for it. All our lives will be. In a way we barely understand, everyone else who comes into our prayers will be blessed by that as well.

> Lord God, remind me of the thrill of being directly in conversation with the creator of the universe. Amen.

And life will be better. It just will! Because you will be living your life in the context of everything that ever was and ever will be. That's what it means to be open to God. And there is only one way for life to go if you take your rightful place in the whole of the existence of everything, and that is up!

In the Bible, when Paul prayed for his friends in Ephesus,

he prayed that they would be stuffed full of Jesus' love. If that happens to you, prayer for everyone you encounter from day to day will bubble out, because that's what a love like Jesus' does for you. Thankfulness will just sparkle out of you – you won't need to wait for a special, hushed moment. You'll confess all that has gone wrong without even needing to be prompted, because you will be genuinely sorry for the smudge you've made on the world that Jesus loves. And you'll be looking to see what God has done to answer your prayer just because you are aware that you are working out his good will in his good world.

> **Be happy!**
> Practise going through tomorrow praying momentarily about all the things that come into view – good or bad, happy or sad, in the news or in the flesh, friend or stranger. Try to persuade others to copy you, and keep it multiplying, so that your neighbourhood becomes a loved place, the source of it being Jesus, rooted deep within you, wide and high and long and deep.

Your street will be blessed; Birmingham will be blessed; maybe the blessing will even reach Uzbekistan. And life will be better. It will. I don't mean there will be no sadness in it. But you will be acutely aware of the joy, and so life will be better.

Fewer rules; more prayers. Fewer questions; more giving it a go. Less reading; more Jesus. Less waffle; more love. And God will do what God will do, and the result will be glory, in the church and in Christ Jesus, throughout all generations, for ever and ever.

Be Happy!
Day 30
Be confident

When she was four, I gave my god-daughter Anna a gold-fish for her birthday. She called it Walter. (Actually, I think she called it Water, but we all jumped to the wrong conclusion. When I visited last week she was calling it something else, so either she changed her mind or the fish has registered a new name by deed poll.)

Anna and I have spent a long time staring at that little golden beauty. 'Is he hungry?'

'I don't know, Anna.'

'Is he lonely?'

'I don't know.'

'Is he hurting?'

'I don't know.'

> Since we have a great high priest who has gone through the heavens, Jesus the Son of God, let us hold firmly to the faith we profess. For we do not have a high priest who is unable to sympathise with our weaknesses, but we have one who has been tempted in every way, just as we are – yet was without sin. Let us then approach the throne of grace with confidence, so that we may receive mercy and find grace to help us in our time of need.
>
> Hebrews 4.14–16

'Why don't you know?'

The truth is, the poor little creature depends totally on that family to stay alive. (The fish, not my god-daughter!) But I have no idea what he really needs; I can only guess. When he opens his mouth like that, is he talking or yawning? The only way I could really address what he needs would be to become a fish and swim around with him for a while.

You have a God who understands every feeling you've ever had. Are you frightened stupid by a relative's life-threatening illness? He appreciates what that's about. Stressed to breaking point by work that's too difficult? God knows. Hopelessly in love with someone else's boyfriend? He knows. No matter how scared, lonely or guilty you feel, God sympathizes unreservedly. Why? Because he has done something as extraordinary as me becoming a goldfish. He has become a human.

Jesus.

That God should inhabit a human body is

> [The Lord said,] 'Here is my servant, whom I uphold, my chosen one in whom I delight;
> I will put my Spirit on him and he will bring justice to the nations.
> He will not shout or cry out, or raise his voice in the streets.
> A bruised reed he will not break, and a smouldering wick he will not snuff out.
> In faithfulness he will bring forth justice; he will not falter or be discouraged till he establishes justice on earth ...
> I, the Lord, have called you in righteousness; I will take hold of your hand.'
>
> *Isaiah 42.1–4, 6*

such a mind-boggling thought that the Bible uses several images to try to explain it (or at least, to help us glimpse what it entails). One of them is to describe Jesus as a priest

> Sometimes we get unduly elated when things go well. At other times we are too dejected when they go badly. What we need is to establish our hearts firmly in God's strength, and struggle as best we can to place all our confidence in him. In this way we shall be like him, as far as is possible, sharing his unchanging rest and his stability.
>
> *Jordan of Saxony, monk and academic, 1190–1237*

– in fact, a high priest. The original readers of the Bible would have understood how significant that was, because a priest was a person who could move comfortably between God and humans, taking the prayers of men and women directly to the presence of God.

The man who described Jesus as a priest wanted his readers to know that Jesus was full of compassion and knew exactly what it felt like to be human. The difference was that priests were (and are) fallible. They were good, but not perfect. So imagine the confidence we can have in a priest who was utterly without fault of any kind. We have such a priest in Jesus Christ. It means that we can pray with certainty that there will be help when we need it. We might fail, but Jesus won't. And that puts you and me in a better position than Walter. A million times better.

Another image that was associated with Christ for hundreds of years before Jesus was even born is God's Servant. Isaiah wrote three wonderful things about this Servant that can make a genuine difference to our lives today.

> Set off on the path of prayer with confidence. Then swiftly and speedily you will reach the place of peace, which is your stronghold against the place of fear.
>
> *Evagrius, monk and writer, known as 'The Solitary', 345–99*

First, he says of the Servant: 'A bruised reed he will not break, and a smouldering wick he will not snuff out.' Jesus has shown us a completely different way from the world's standards. In a godless world, when you mess up, you're lost. If you're weak, you're at the back of the queue. If you fail you're on your own, mate!

But Jesus, the one who walked on this earth beside us, is different. If you see yourself as a candle that is spluttering and failing, no matter whether everyone else in the world would snuff you out and start with a new one, the way of Jesus is to tend the wick, reshape the wax, cajole the flame back into life, and persist with what is valuable in you until it comes alive again. 'A smouldering wick he will not snuff out.' The image of the bruised reed, not chopped down but coaxed back into fruitfulness, means the same. You don't get that kind of care in a godless world. Be confident, for this Jesus is your God.

> Jesus Christ, Son of God, Saviour, take my hand and lead me. Amen.

The second thing that Isaiah says of the Servant is: 'Faithfully he will bring forth justice. He will not falter, he will not be discouraged until he establishes justice.' In a godless world, humans become worth whatever value they can reach in the market place. If you're poor, you're taken for whatever you can be exploited for. If you're rich, you become obsessed by the bargain you can get in the shop and blinded to the appalling conditions some worker in the southern hemisphere endures so that you get things cheap.

But Jesus, the one who talked on this earth among us, is one in whom the poor can put their hope, because he works for justice. And he is also one whom the rich can trust, for he can release them from the burden of always wanting more. He has come, Isaiah wrote, 'to open eyes that are blind, to free captives from prison, and to release from the dungeon those who sit in darkness.' You don't get that kind of determination to do what is right in a godless world. Be confident, for this Jesus is your God.

Last, and most personally, Isaiah puts wonderful promises in the mouth of God: 'I, the righteous Lord, have called you. I will take hold of your hand. I will keep you.' This is the kind of God you have. Not a distant God towards whom you stumble optimistically. Not a ferocious God in light so dazzling that it would burn you up if you tried to approach. Not a messenger who points the way and leaves you to do what you think is best. At least, not *just* those things. You have a God who is walking and talking alongside you on every step of the confusing path through a difficult world. In one hand he is holding a lamp giving just precisely as much light as you need to make the next move. And in the other hand he is holding your hand. Be confident, for this Jesus is your God.

> ### Be happy!
> Slowly and imaginatively, foresee what you expect to be doing in one hour's time; in twelve hours; a month ahead; a year ahead. In each case, picture yourself in that setting with Jesus gripping you supportively by the hand. Tell him your feelings about what you see and get ready to tackle the circumstances confidently.

That is an awful lot of good news to be taught by one goldfish. But I am happy to say that I am not the first person to compare Jesus to a fish. That image first appears in the art that decorates the catacombs of Rome – the huge complex of underground galleries excavated by Christians in the soft stone outside the city. This is where grieving Christians, from about one hundred years after Jesus died, buried their relatives and friends, in sure and confident hope that they would meet again in the presence of God.

Why a fish? It was a simple and memorable image, of course, which could easily be scratched in the dust as a secret sign between fearful believers. But it was also a code. The initial letters of the Greek words *Iesous CHristos THeou Uios Soter* spell *ichthus*, which means fish. And what do those tongue-twisting words mean? They mean 'Jesus Christ, the Son of God, the Saviour'.

A fish told those Christians in Rome all they needed to know about the one in whom they had put their trust. It gave them confidence in life, and it allowed them to let go confidently into death. I pray that this will be your experience too.

Be Happy!
Day 31
Hope!

I met a woman called Hope. Everyone called her Esperanza, because this was in the Dominican Republic, and I was visiting to find out about the work of Onè Respé (the charity I wrote about on Day 12). But I had a translator with me, so I know what her name means.

> I pray also that the eyes of your heart may be enlightened in order that you may know the hope to which [God] has called you, the riches of his glorious inheritance in the saints, and his incomparably great power for us who believe. That power is like the working of his mighty strength, which he exerted in Christ when he raised him from the dead and seated him at his right hand in the heavenly realms.
>
> *Ephesians 1.18–20*

Hope told me her moving story at the clinic, which is one of the few places on the island where the poorest inhabitants know that they will not be turned away: 'Onè Respé has been my mum. More than that – God has arrived! Onè Respé has a heart like God's. I could never give back what I have received from them, but they will be repaid in heaven. People treat me with love here. Other people say, "Don't eat with that woman. She's got HIV, but it's worse

173

than that – she's Haitian too." But here it is totally different. I feel I am . . .' She stretched out her arms and wrapped them around herself in a hug. Then she roared with laughter.

'My blood is bad. There is a lot of pain which comes and goes. I have lesions and I am sore all over.' At this point she stood up and took off her shirt to show me how bad the spots were. Being the person on the entire island who is least used to women taking their clothes off in front of him, I was not exactly sure how close an examination was appropriate without seeming impolite. I found myself murmuring, 'Oh, my word!' Then I felt ridiculous, because I sounded like a character from a P. G. Wodehouse story. So I added, 'I'm so sorry.'

> May the God of hope fill you with all joy and peace as you trust in him, so that you may overflow with hope by the power of the Holy Spirit.
>
> Romans 15.13

'I have had the virus for four years. At first I couldn't stop crying. But then Onè Respé gave me a bed so that I don't have to sleep on the floor. It was the first caring thing that anyone had done for me. Now I have been given a radio as well, so I am able to think about other things apart from my illness. I feel much more hopeful.'

> Do not be surprised, my child, and do not lose hope. I too, old and grey as I am, am still much troubled by bad thoughts. Do not be discouraged by such burning desires, for they are healed not so much by human effort as by God's compassion.
>
> Apollo, Egyptian desert father (hermit), about 300–50

And then, without warning, she burst into tears – huge sobs. Everyone in the room went to Hope and hugged her. Even my translator! But I stood back by the door having no idea what to do in this situation. I found I was stretching my arms out, uselessly hugging empty air. I felt ineffectual and naive and so pathetically British. I felt that I was being given something precious by a noble person, and did not know how to accept the gift.

She went on, 'I am alone here in the Dominican Republic. I don't have a husband or children. I had to move out of Los Platinos because people would not stop insulting me, so now I am a squatter on a construction site. What I really want to do is work. I've been a cleaner in someone's house in the past; I could do that again.

'I pray that God will change my heart. I want him to stop me thinking bad things about others. Sometimes I have bad thoughts and want to harm the people who have hurt me so much. I plead with God to take my bad thoughts away. Only he can change a person's heart.'

And then the mood turned again with barely a moment's notice.

'At the Onè Respé women's group I learnt to make pots. Then I learnt how to write my name. But that's not the important thing – I have received love. I'm not treated like a dog, but like a real human. All these people are good deep down in their hearts. I don't know how to give back what I have received.'

Hope is one of the great themes of the Bible. When Paul uses the word, it is to distinguish those who have put their faith in Jesus from those who haven't. It's not something that can be measured or held or seen – it needs to be sensed deep down with what Paul calls 'the eyes of your heart'.

> Strike that thick cloud of unknowing with the sharp dart of longing love, and on no account whatever think of giving up.
>
> The Cloud of Unknowing, *an anonymous spiritual guidebook from England, about 1370*

So what does it mean? It's easier to say what it *doesn't* mean. It isn't a vague sense of hoping for the best but not actually having a clue (which is what we usually mean when we use the word). I hope it's going to be sunny next Saturday because I'm going to a wedding. But I don't know whether it will be, and there is no way I can influence it one way or another. I just have to sit and wait with crossed fingers. That's not what a Christian means when he or she talks about hope.

But on the other hand, Christian hope is not a certainty. It deals in things that can't be proved. I have heard people say, 'I am absolutely certain beyond any doubt that there will be a life after death.' But I don't honestly see how it is possible to be certain about things like that. It's a matter of faith, not of proof. If it were possible to be certain then everyone in the world would be believers and, very evidently, not everyone is.

> Lord God, even if they take everything else away from me, never let them take away my hope. Amen.

Don't get me wrong! I have come to the conclusion that there is a God, that we will meet him, and that there will be a glorious future beyond our life on earth. But I can't prove it and so it would be foolish to say that it's a certainty. So that's not what hope means either.

Hope means having a calm and settled state of mind that assumes in everything, from the big decisions to the smallest, that we can rely on God. It is a confidence that we can trust him for all the things about which it is impossible to be certain. And it is life-transforming. It means that when we have doubts about what we believe or what we should do, they come in the context of assuming that we have a good God who wants the best for us, and is preparing for us an eternity that is incomparably rich. Paul calls it 'the riches of his glorious inheritance in the saints'. How thrilling is that! It can give us courage to endure loss, disappointment and sadness with a quiet trust that we are loved by and safe in the hands of God.

There is a reason why we can have that calm and settled confidence in God, which refuses to be daunted by uncertainty. Our hope in the future is rooted in a God who knows the way of a grave. Our God is the resurrection God.

The power that raised Jesus from the dead is also the power that sustained courageous faith while lions were roaring in the coliseum; subservient faith when kings stepped up to the throne for their coronation; glorious faith when communion was consecrated in a grand cathedral; committed faith by a believer at his baptism; nervous faith by a student about to sit her exams; exploratory faith by a young man leaving home for the first time; thankful faith from someone who survived cancer; angry faith at the funeral of someone who didn't; desperate faith by a nation on whom bombs were dropping; anxious faith by a mother wondering why her daughter is not yet home from the nightclub at three in the morning; sustained faith by a couple enjoying their golden wedding anniversary; joyous faith by a band singing, 'He has risen, he has risen, Jesus is alive!'

Having a hope like this has made me sincerely content. I pray that you will be able to share it. The preachers did their best to encourage it by explaining the Bible to me. But I don't think I understood it fully until I learnt it in a whitewashed clinic in the Caribbean from a woman called Hope. Viva Esperanza!

> Be happy!
> Explore the website of a charity that works to bring human hope. The one described in this chapter is at www.onerespe.com. Click on the link to the English language version of the site, or use a search engine's translation function.

Be Happy!

Day 32

Value friends

I am writing this chapter on a train from London to Cornwall. I am on my way to the most south-westerly corner of England. There are two teenagers opposite me. They have been kissing each other without a break from Exeter to Truro. It started off as annoying, but now it is becoming phenomenal. It's an 87-mile snog. When the train manager prised them apart to check their tickets it was like a sink plunger parting company with a plughole.

> One who has many companions may come to ruin, but there is a friend who sticks closer than a brother or sister.
>
> *Proverbs 18.24*

The guy has got four tattoos that I can see. (Now is not an appropriate moment to ask whether he has others.) The one on his arm has inspired me for the subject of this chapter – in curly letters it reads 'forever friends'. There is no way of knowing whether it is dedicated to the girl. However, I can't help noticing that she hasn't looked at him for the last sixty minutes. She has been staring past his cheek and out of the window, watching the countryside rattle by. She really does not seem to have any interest in him at all. He has two little teardrops inked into the skin at the corner of his eye, and I find myself wondering whether there is such a thing as a prophetic tattoo. All my pastoral instincts are engaged. I wish I could offer them some relationship counselling now that they could keep on file for when they need it in the future. Unfortunately, though, friendship doesn't work like that.

What I most want to tell these two young people is that 'forever friends' is an idea that has ancient roots in the Bible, but that the time-filling kiss to which you are not particularly committed is a much more recent invention. The Bible is endlessly positive about the value of friendship, but the most famous kiss in the Bible was a betrayal.

It is not friendliness that the Bible encourages; it's friendship. To have a friend is different from having a band of people you hang around with, different from having an entertaining work colleague, different from having a sexual relationship or a family tie. All those things are good, but there is a unique goodness about friendship that can strengthen the other relationships. The Bible shows it taking place between two men (for instance, Jonathan and David, who had devotion to God in common), between two women (Ruth and Naomi, whose friendship crossed religions and generations, and sustained them through tragedy), and between men and women (such as Jesus' friendship with Martha and Mary, in whose home he could effortlessly relax).

> Two are better than one, because they have a good return for their work. If one falls down, a friend can help the other up. But pity those who fall and have no friend to help them up!
>
> *Ecclesiastes 4.9–10*

> Keep company with the more cheerful sort of the godly; there is no mirth like the mirth of believers.
>
> *Richard Baxter, church leader and writer, 1615–91*

Friendship is never going to offer the rich happiness of which the Bible speaks unless time is invested in it. To say this runs counter to the culture of the twenty-first century because the internet has encouraged people to describe themselves as friends when their contact takes place merely by watching a computer monitor. Facebook relationships offer friendliness (which is not a bad thing, but is limited); face-to-face relationships offer friendship. You know when you have created a friendship of true value when you discover that you have received more pleasure from meeting than the effort you put into making it happen – and realize that the other person has had the same experience. Curiously, friendship does not involve give and take – in a way that surmounts tiredness and stress, the giving turns out to be the taking. One of the Bible's sayings puts it like this: 'Two are better than one, because they have a good return for their work.' But it goes on to say: 'Pity those who fall and have no friend to help them up.'

How do you get a friend like that? It is not a matter of luck, and it will not happen if you sit in a lonely place in the hope that someone will come to you. It involves taking yourself where people with whom you are likely to have common interests congregate, and engaging with all sorts

> No medicine is more valuable ... than a friend. He will be someone whose soul will be to us a refuge to creep into when the world is altogether too much for us, and someone to whom we can confide all our thoughts. His spirit will give us the comforting kiss that heals all the sickness of our preoccupied hearts. He will weep with us when we are troubled, and rejoice when we are happy. He will always be there to consult when we are in doubt. And we will be so deeply bound to him in our hearts that even when he is far away we shall find him together with us in spirit.
>
> *Aelred of Rievaulx, monk and writer, 1110–67*

of men and women. Not every person you speak to will become a lifelong friend, but those are the circumstances in which individuals with whom you share values and hopes at a deep level emerge from a crowd.

Imposing yourself on people seizes their attention, but not their affection. The best way to gain a friend is to offer yourself as one, and then wait for the invitation to be accepted. I have tended to find that if you crack jokes you will impress people, but if you laugh at other people's jokes they will thoroughly enjoy your company. Am I the only one who has experienced that?

Friendship usually grows gradually, and is a matter of increasingly becoming more open to each other. To be honest, nobody wants to hear about the catastrophic failings of your life on the first occasion they meet you. However, growing confidence in a friend allows you to talk about your aspirations and your disappointments, feeling lighter in spirit because of having been able to say these things in the knowledge that someone has listened and understood.

> Loving God, make me a loyal friend and give me a loyal friend. And may the result be that burdens are halved and pleasures are doubled. Amen.

The need for confidentiality is vital at these times – if things that were meant to be private seep out, it will ruin your friendship. However, a true friendship is one in which there can be frankness as well. (If a good friend tells you that he or she is considering being unfaithful to a spouse, the proper response is not 'Do you need an alibi?'; it is, 'You pillock!') All these modern-sounding truths have been sitting in the scriptures for 3,000 years waiting for this moment: 'Wounds from a friend can be trusted, but an enemy multiplies kisses,' wrote the wise man of Proverbs. And he went on: 'Perfume and incense bring joy to the heart, and the pleasantness of one's friends springs from their earnest counsel.'

Only a friendship in which people appreciate each other at a deep level can thrive under circumstances in which honest, uncomfortable advice is given. The circumstances in which it is acceptable are fostered over a substantial period of time, during which there has been care, acceptance and respect. Perhaps the most valuable thing that friends can give each other is affirmation. It is a powerful boost to your self-esteem to experience someone telling you what they admire or enjoy about you, either directly or by implying it. Don't wait for that to happen! Take the initiative in making it a feature of your friendships. You don't need to make an embarrassing or drunken speech – just slide it into the conversation and then change the subject. But don't take your friendships for granted. Work at them, and you will find the investment repays itself in happiness, in a desire to be a better person, and in an increased strength in your family relationships or marriage.

> **Be happy!**
> Who would appreciate a phone call?

We have reached Truro and the young couple have left the train. It is a cold evening, and on the platform the boy takes off his jacket and puts it round the girl's shoulders. It is such an old-fashioned and gentlemanly thing to do that my heart goes out to them both. She says something to him that I can't hear from the other side of the glass, but it is evidently full of affection. I think I may have leapt to the wrong conclusions earlier. I shall be praying for them last thing tonight.

Oh, heaven help us, they're at it again! Take me to Land's End.

A happy future

Be Happy!

Day 33

Accept sadness

I could write about any country or any person in the world in order to reflect on sadness. It is universal. No human life is or could be spared it entirely. But as soon as I had decided on the title, I knew I wanted to write about Sri Lanka. It is an island in South Asia that sits like a tear dropping from the south coast of India.

Perhaps it is the world's most beautiful island. High in the hills the tea bushes stretch in bright green lines as if the steeps have been combed for inspection. By the coast the sand is as fine as golden flour. Cows wander through the towns, past shops with eccentric names (one advertises 'prosthetic limbs, fax and photocopying'). In the lakes, islands rise into absurd cones of yellow flowers, as if God

> [Jesus said,] 'I tell you the truth, you will weep and mourn while the world rejoices. You will grieve, but your grief will turn to joy. A woman giving birth to a child has pain because her time has come; but when her baby is born she forgets the anguish because of her joy that a child is born into the world. So with you: Now is your time of grief, but I will see you again and you will rejoice, and no-one will take away your joy.
>
> John 16.20–22

> Be merciful to me, O Lord, for I am in distress;
> my eyes grow weak with sorrow,
> my soul and my body with grief.
> My life is consumed by anguish and my years by groaning;
> my strength fails because of my affliction ...
> But I trust in you, O Lord; I say, 'You are my God.'
> My times are in your hands;
> deliver me from my enemies and from those who pursue me.
> Let your face shine on your servant;
> save me in your unfailing love.
>
> *Psalm 31.9–10, 14–16*

has tipped blooms from a vast salt cellar and, thrilled by his own naughtiness, cannot bring himself to stop pouring until the whole pot is empty.

The people of Sri Lanka have endured overwhelming sadness during recent decades. There have been nearly thirty years of civil war, a tsunami caused shocking devastation in 2004, and the crippling poverty associated with both of these has been exacerbated by the oppression of first one ethnic group and then another in grievances that stretch back into the island's colonial history. It is, however, the way ordinary men and women have dealt with their sadness that is the country's inspiring story.

That is true of Valliami, made destitute when her village was burnt to the ground by soldiers who wrongly thought that enemy guerrillas were hiding there. Demeaned by having to scavenge and sell firewood, she sought a loan of 1,000 rupees from Thadaham, a superb organization supported by money given by Christians in the UK. She used it to buy a share in a rice-processing machine, and paid off the loan. She grouped together with other women to create a business, began to work her way out of poverty, sent her children to school, and now lives in a rebuilt village with, for the first time, a well.

One thousand rupees is £6. That is the kind of sum that can enable someone in the developing world to turn their life around. Six quid! Think of that next time you buy a cinema ticket!

In the island's theological college I met Gnanarajah Manozuban – good-looking and earnest. 'All of us are human beings,' he said to me. 'We are separated by language and divisions. But every one of us is human, so I want to see God's image in your face.'

> There are as many nights as days. Even a happy life cannot be without a measure of darkness, and the word 'happy' would lose its meaning if it were not balanced by sadness.
>
> *Carl Jung, psychologist, 1875–1961*

Knowing that he was training to be a clergyman, I asked him what had led him to this point. 'I am here because of the great sadness of my family,' he replied. 'When I was thirteen I was hit by a shell from an enemy gun. May I show you?' He lowered the side of his trousers, and revealed a hole three centimetres deep in his hip. 'My mother was weeping. All our neighbours said, "Where is your God now?" The Red Cross took me to hospital. The doctor said I wouldn't be able to walk for a year. But I was determined. I walked again after twenty-two days. Then I knew where my God was.

> Strengthen your patience with understanding, and look forward serenely to the joy that comes after sadness.
>
> *Peter Damian, Italian church leader, 1007–72*

'That is what leads me to train for ordination. It is not enough for me to say thank you to God with my prayers; I need to say thank you with my whole life. I would like to say to the man who did this to me, "You must never do this again. I want to be a

Christian who forgives and forgets. I know that I have forgiven you. If you never do it again I will eventually forget as well, but I find that much harder."'

I learnt so much about how to deal with sadness from the people I met in Sri Lanka. One thing I learnt was that although it is natural to ask, 'Why me?' it is a question from which we all need to move on. There may be an answer to the question, because sometimes we must honestly confront the fact that we have brought sadness on ourselves. But more often there is no answer, and pursuing it endlessly prevents pain from healing. Why the bereavement, why the divorce, why the failure of ambitions? Truly and sincerely I want to tell you this – you do not have sadness in your life because God has picked you out to suffer it. Sadness is a state through which every one of us must go, whether it passes quickly or burrows deep. It is the way the world has been established for all humankind, not specifically because God is angry with you.

Despite your secret fears, God loves you and is leading you through your most depressed moments into a future in which happiness is possible. One of the psalms puts it like this: 'God's anger lasts only a moment, but his favour lasts a lifetime; weeping may remain for a night, but rejoicing comes in the morning.' This does not mean there is nothing to learn from what has happened to you, especially if you need to take responsibility for ensuring you never repeat a mistake. But try to recognize this as a way of moving on, not a reason to revisit bad experiences over and over again – as Gnanarajah is genuinely struggling to do.

> OK God. I have lived through unhappy times. But I won't wallow, I won't blame you, and I won't despair. I have no idea how I'm going to get out of this mess. But it's you and me together now. Please don't let me down. Amen.

There are many other things that I learnt in Sri Lanka. I learnt that it is nonsense to tell children that big boys don't cry. Or girls for that matter! Grief needs an expression, particularly when love has been lost, whatever the cause. Weeping is part of recovery, and sitting without embarrassment next to someone tearful is one of the ways of offering them healing on their long journey to recovery.

I also learnt the importance of the story being told. Those who have lived through misery, such as traumatic violence, need to bear witness to what they have seen and experienced in order to reach a point at which events that have shaped their past no longer command control of their future. In the same way, albeit with less intensity, we all need someone to whom we can talk about the sorrow inside us – not looking for advice, but seeking understanding. For those who are deeply depressed there are professional listeners, and no one should hold back from seeking this kind of help if they need it. But far more people simply need someone who knows when to speak and when to listen; when to take time and when to pray.

> **Be happy!**
> Make some decisions about the parts of your life that weigh you down with sadness – talk about them, cry about them, pray about them, get busy with alternatives to them. In fact, do anything except wallow in them.

Finally, I learnt how positive action can accelerate the pace at which you move on from distress into composure. If your life has interests or work, relationships or plans, the journey out of sadness is easier. (I don't mean reckless overwork, which is a way of numbing unhappiness instead of progressing through it to a better place; rather I mean being comfortably busy.) Valliami, a devout Hindu who turned her distress into determination to resurrect her community, impressed this on me: 'We would gladly give our lives for the people who helped us [borrow the resources to rebuild our village], because they were the only ones who cared a jot for us.'

I would like to be remembered as one of those who cared a jot. I believe it will help me accept sadness next time it visits me as part of my happy life.

Be Happy!

Day 34

Set goals

I went to my godchildren's school to see their nativity play. *Christmas in Hawaii*. Anna played a hula-hula girl. (Don't ask! Me neither!) That show had everything! It had song, it had dance, it had spectacle. It had children stopping mid-sentence to wave to their parents. It had more flash photography than a celebrity premiere. And it had Joseph lifting up his costume and showing the audience his pants. What a night in the theatre! You'd pay fifty quid for that in the West End.

> Forgetting what is behind and straining towards what is ahead, I press on towards the goal to win the prize for which God has called me heavenward in Christ Jesus. All of us who are mature should take such a view of things.
>
> *Philippians 3.13–15*

I was incredibly proud and happy, then at the end I was suddenly very moved. Anna was singing 'Away in a Manger'. (You see, they did get to Bethlehem eventually!) I've always loved that carol, and had never really worked out why. But as Anna sang her solo I listened more intently than usual, and I realized why. It's the last line: 'And fit us for heaven to live with thee there.'

I had one of those moments of clarity when you think,

191

yes of course, that's what the whole shebang is about. That's precisely what we are here on this planet for – to be made fit to live with Jesus in eternity. It's why Jesus was born on earth. He has shown us the whole point of being a human. There it is, made absolutely plain in the words of a song that I have known since I was four. Or probably even earlier – I've known that truth for so long that I've no memory of how I came to know it.

> To human beings belong the plans of the heart, but from the Lord comes the reply of the tongue ... Commit to the Lord whatever you do, and your plans will succeed ... In your heart you may plan your course, but the Lord determines your steps.
>
> *Proverbs 16.1, 3, 9*

It's not giving away a big secret to say that I love Christmas. Always have! I even love the commercialized, tacky tat that crams the shop windows and the TV channels. Yup, that's how shallow I am!

The day after the nativity play I was in the supermarket, and next to the mince pies a ridiculously overexcited child was having a tantrum over not being able to have a yoghurt with Scooby Doo on it. And a man said to me, 'Ooh, I flippin' hate Christmas, don't you?'

I said, 'You're telling the wrong bloke, mate – I love it!' I was swamped with a light-headed joy at the fact that it was *that* time of year, and I ran with my trolley up

> Be near me, Lord Jesus, I ask thee to stay Close by me for ever, and love me I pray. Bless all the dear children in thy tender care, And fit us for heaven, to live with thee there.
>
> *William Kirkpatrick, hymn writer, 1838–1921*

the aisle and jumped on the back of it. And a kid doing a Saturday job came up and said, 'Excuse me, sir, that's not allowed in this store.' I thought, 'What's happening to the world? Old men hate Christmas and I'm being told off by a fourteen–year-old schoolboy!'

Christmas is the only time in the year when we are absolutely surrounded by Christian symbols. Angels come and take up their stations on lampposts. Stars guide our way, hovering in light over the trees. What a blessing! It doesn't happen during the other eleven months of the year. It's as if we are surrounded by the goodness of God, and choosing not to notice it. Of course, you have to hunt for God among the tat – but that's how the Christian faith is. It always has been, from the very first. Even the writer of John's Gospel complained about it: Jesus 'was in the world, and though the world was made through him, the world did not recognize him'.

It takes practice to look constantly for God in action in a world that seems to be ignoring him. But that is what

> All the life that has been given back to me has not been mine in the full sense; it is built around a purpose.
>
> *Alexander Solzhenitsyn, Christian dissident and survivor of the Gulag, the Soviet Union's forced labour camps, who went on to be a Nobel prize-winning writer, 1918–2008*

is required if we are to live in a way that is preparing us for heaven, the destination to which all human activity is leading. And our aspirations in life all depend on that preparation if pursuing them is to bring us happiness, rather than disappointment.

Dreams are not, by themselves, enough. Dreams need targets, targets need strategies, and strategies need resolve in order to fulfil them. There are no short cuts, I'm sorry to say. Aspirations are so often frustrated by the fact that it is easy to put off action until the moment you feel like starting – a moment that never comes. Many things can contribute to this – the legacy of careless words by a teacher, the example of parents who never reached their potential, or a mind that cannot see its way through the dozen tasks that need doing to find the one that should come first. Any of these can give you a fear of starting something because another failure would be so disheartening. But all can be overcome – with partnership, with advice, or just with grit.

Set goals and targets! Write them down, if necessary. Be realistic, but don't be diffident. If you need to lose some weight, achieving the size that your doctor recommends will make you look and (more importantly) feel beautiful. But fancying yourself as a supermodel will leave you as pitiful as a pipe-cleaner. If your home is a mess, tidying and cleaning one room will give you sufficient satisfaction to tackle another; applying to appear on a television programme that shows a house being decorated in a day doesn't count as a target!

> Enough excuses, Lord! I am getting on with things. Help me find the resources to achieve my goals. Amen.

There is more to a goal than longing. A goal is longing plus organization; it needs to be something that you yourself can control. It can be financial (such as paying off a debt), emotional (such as having a bit of adventure in a dull period of your life), or intellectual (such as achieving a new qualification). None of these appears particularly spiritual – and of course, God will not like you one scrap less or more if you realize them. But the sense of accomplishment that follows will excite you about being alive. This is what God wants for all his followers, and it will make you ready to meet him with great relish. It will call you heavenward, as Paul described it in the Bible. He was writing about how the desire to be united with Jesus in a never-ending friendship had transformed the way he pressed forward through life.

Whatever your target is, you will need a strategy for how you are going to fulfil it. A strategy is not meant to be a straitjacket – you can reform your plans if they are not working as well as you hoped, or if something unexpected happens. And New Year's Day is probably the worst moment to start your strategy, since a new year's resolution is something people do because they feel they ought to, not because they have a genuine inner drive to do it. A good moment to begin is usually now. Involve friends and helpers, summon all your resolve, and start now! Don't let negativity interrupt you, don't allow feelings to slow you down, don't let little failures daunt you from pressing on!

Stop dreaming of a white Christmas; get out the whitewash and roll up your sleeves! Set yourself a goal, make a plan or a timetable for how you will achieve it, and gather up the determination to get going. And then, as you realize that your aspiration is going to be fulfilled, you'll have a sudden rush of delight. You'll be standing in a supermarket with a shopping trolley in your hands and an empty aisle will open up in front of you . . .

Go on! I dare you!

Be happy!

Make a strategy about how to achieve something that you have been meaning to do for a while. It could be something small that improves your home or something with a long-lasting legacy that will change your circumstances. Plan to take the first step to achieve your goal before a week has gone by, so that at the end of this spiritual journey you will have the joy of knowing that something definite is under way. If a particular goal has come to mind, write a note at the end of this chapter so that you will have extra satisfaction when it is fulfilled.

Be Happy!

Day 35

Pass it on

My godchildren are an almost inexhaustible source of happiness for me. At eight, Anna already has leadership qualities that Joan of Arc would envy. Two years younger, William is the kindest little boy I have known. On Boxing Day we were exchanging Christmas presents, and as William opened the DVD I gave him, Mum shot me a look to warn me that it was one he already owned. But as I was thinking what to say to make it all right, he said, 'Hooray! Now we've got two!'

> [Timothy,] I thank God, whom I serve, as my forefathers did, with a clear conscience, as night and day I constantly remember you in my prayers. Recalling your tears, I long to see you, so that I may be filled with joy. I have been reminded of your sincere faith, which first lived in your grandmother Lois and in your mother Eunice and, I am persuaded, now lives in you also. For this reason I remind you to fan into flame the gift of God, which is in you through the laying on of my hands. For God did not give us a spirit of timidity, but a spirit of power, of love and of self-discipline.
>
> 2 Timothy 1.3–7

I thought that was so lovely of him, because aged six he dug me out of an embarrassing situation that grown adults struggle to deal with. Where has that kindness come from? He didn't decide to begin to act like that last Boxing Day. Children don't do things for no reason. Their actions are the result of what they have experienced during the previous four, six, twelve, twenty years. The characteristics I see in Anna and William are those I can trace to their mother and father. I have known Dad since he himself was about Anna's age. I was his teacher.

Today's chapter is about how happiness can be passed on to the next generation. The example that springs to my mind is a young man called Timothy, whose memory is kept alive in the New Testament. People grew up a lot quicker in the first century, and of course, died a lot younger. So at a frighteningly young age, Timothy was already leading a church in Ephesus. It was a church founded by Apollos, strengthened by Paul, thriving because of the Holy Spirit, and then left for Timothy to head up.

> May your father and mother be glad; may she who gave you birth rejoice!
> *Proverbs 23.25*

Three key people brought Timothy to the point at which he was capable (rather frightened, but capable) of leading the church. A grandparent, a parent, and an older adult who was not related but was deeply involved.

The older adult was Paul, and a great deal is known about him. But almost nothing is known about Eunice, Timothy's mother, or Lois, his grandmother. Eunice was Jewish and then adopted Christianity. She must have been a pious Jew, because she taught Timothy the Bible (our Old Testament) from an early age. She was married to a Gentile, so I guess this was not the easiest thing, but it does give hope to families today in which one parent is a faithful worshipper but the other does not show the same commitment.

There is even more guessing when it comes to Lois. I suppose the two women had their children aged about thirteen or fourteen, so Lois must have been a contemporary of Jesus, but she lived in Lystra; she too became one of his followers. Paul had anxieties about the Christian church being hijacked by heretical teachers and going into decline, but he need not have feared. The church was going to become the biggest world-shaping force for good that history has seen. And, in the goodness of God, two virtually unknown and insignificant women were crucial to that happening. Not because they had ambitions to be high-flying movers and shakers, but because they brought up a little boy to be a faithful follower of the Lord Jesus. That's wonderful!

> There is just one way to bring up a child in the way he should go, and that is to travel that way yourself.
>
> Abraham Lincoln, sixteenth President of the USA, 1809–65

It's wonderful because this is where you and I fit into the unfolding story of what God intends for the planet – we will be unknown in history, but crucial in passing on the faith that we have inherited as the clearest way to make sense of our extraordinary world.

How do we do that? Through what we say, but even more through the example that children see. Chil-

> Give me the children until they are seven, and anyone may have them afterwards.
>
> Francis Xavier, Jesuit teacher and missionary in India, 1505–52

dren copy. They see, they think about it, they try things out, they see if it fits the world-view they are developing, they create a version of it that seems good to them, and then they copy some more. That's what happened to Timothy, and it still does!

So be careful what's copied! The minister had been invited to Sunday lunch by a family in the congregation. Dad asked him to say grace, but the minister boomed, 'Why don't we let your young son Jackie say grace?'

Jack froze: 'I don't know what to say.'

'That's all right,' said Mum. 'Just copy exactly what Daddy said to God at breakfast this morning.'

'Oh, that's easy,' said the boy, shutting his eyes tight. 'O God, is it today that boring old man's coming to lunch?'

May I suggest some better things for children to copy? Paul's ideas, not mine: 'God did not give us a spirit of timidity, but a spirit of power, of love and of self-discipline.'

> Lord God, I know that the children who are special to me are reading my life as if it were a book. With all my heart, I pray that the book I am writing for them will have a happy ending.
> Amen.

Power, love, self-discipline. If those are the things that the Holy Spirit wants to develop in young people so that they will grow up happy, then those are also three things that we can be involved in building.

Power, because we don't want children to grow up timid. We want them to grow independent, making their way through the world with a strong sense of their worth in it. The way we talk to them, the way we give them opportunities, the way we excite them about the possibilities that the world offers – all these give us a chance to show that to rely on God is genuinely empowering.

Love, because children who grow up knowing beyond doubt that they are loved by someone come to expect that giving love is the way to get the best out of the world. This is something that cannot be taught, only experienced. It will be challenged, tested and exasperated – but it is at those moments that the true, lasting nature of love is demonstrated. That is the context children need if they are to see that the dangerous and suffering world in which we live is under the control of a good God.

And finally, self-discipline. If we are teaching children what it means to have a life of power and a life of love, they also need to work out the balance between the two. They need to have the skills to work out the difference between what's right and what's easy. They need to know how not to get so carried away by the excitement that comes in a bottle, or a relationship, or an ambition achieved, that it grows out of proportion in their life.

Who, then, is the giver of faith to the next generation? God is. Not you or me, but God. Some parents, grandparents and godparents faithfully represent these wonderful qualities to those who come after them, but do not live to see the children adopt faith in the Lord Jesus. It is so important in those circumstances not to feel a failure. Faith is in the gift of God, not you or me. Early influences do not go away. They remain in people, even when they don't get outwardly expressed in a worshipping soul. Like Paul, never lose your hope or relax in your prayer. It is God's job to set a young person's spirituality on fire. We can trust that he knows what he is doing. And our job? To fan that flame.

> **Be happy!**
> If you recognize the relationship between Lois, Eunice, Paul and Timothy as having echoes in your life, do something about it. Grandparent, parent, friend, whatever! Do something particularly if you are a godparent, because that is a relationship that involves promises, and if you haven't kept them as well as you meant to there is no harm in starting now. Write a letter, make a phone call, type an email, send a text message – whatever will be received as a happy surprise.

'Fan into flame the gift of God!' That's what you are doing. And God, who has brought this glorious, life-giving, world-enriching faith through two thousand years will lead us all safely onward through another two, two thousand, two million, whatever it will be until he takes us into his presence with irrepressible joy.

Be Happy!

Day 36

Endure the crisis

Here's a vision for you. Take yourself there! Green, rolling hills. Verdant countryside on a lazy day, with your eyes drifting dreamily towards the undulating horizon. The glorious peaks on a warm afternoon during which there is not a care in the world! You there?

Good! I thought I would give you a chance to daydream for a few seconds because that's absolutely nothing to do with the subject of this chapter. We all deserve a bit of escapism from time to time, but I don't really think that the Christian faith is the best setting to retreat from reality. That isn't going to help us much when we have real difficulties to face. Or real decisions or real deadlines.

I mention this because someone told me last week that Psalm 121 was their favourite psalm because of its vision of peaceful hills, rosy sunsets and endur-

> I lift up my eyes to the hills
> – where does my help come from?
> My help comes from the Lord, the Maker of heaven and earth.
> He will not let your foot slip – he who watches over you will not slumber;
> indeed, he who watches over Israel will neither slumber nor sleep.
>
> *Psalm 121.1–4*

ing calm. Lovely thought – very English, if you don't mind me saying so!

Now, suppose you are an Israelite villager 1,000 years before Jesus was born, at the time when this psalm was written. Your attention has been drawn to something lurking on the distant hills. What thought is going to spring into your mind in those circumstances? Quite clearly, the first word to come out of your mouth will be 'Heeeeeeelp!'

The thing is, the psalms weren't written in the English home counties. They were written in the Middle East at a time when life was grim, brutal and short. And the sight on the hilltop which has unexpectedly caught your eye is the massing horde of an enemy army – maybe Philistines. They are mobilizing to stampede into the valley, destroy your village, kill your men and rape your women. So try to see

> The Lord watches over you
> – the Lord is your shade at your right hand;
> the sun will not harm you by day, nor the moon by night.
> The Lord will keep you from all harm – he will watch over your life;
> the Lord will watch over your coming and going both now and for evermore.
>
> *Psalm 121.5–8*

the opening of the psalm in its original context – through the eyes of a terrified Israelite farmer. 'I lift up my eyes to the hills.' Holy cow! Who on earth is going to help me now? This is not a psalm to take with you to a picnic, this is a psalm to take with you to a crisis.

Christians walk the same paths and stumble into the same emergencies as everyone else. Of course they do! But there is a big difference. Christians know that they are not at the mercy of some random fate. Christians know that they are under the watchful concern of the creator of all things, visible and invisible. So when a crisis arises, we

> The power of God to preserve me; the hand of God to protect me; the way of God to direct me; the shield of God to defend me; the host of God to guard me against the snares of the evil one and the temptations of the world. Christ be with me, Christ above me, Christ within me, Christ before me, Christ in crisis, Christ in danger, Christ I place, by God's almighty grace, between myself and all the powers of darkness.
>
> *Patrick, missionary to Ireland, 389–461*

know precisely what to do first. Who the heck is going to help me this time? The writer of the psalm knew: 'My help comes from the Lord, the Maker of heaven and earth.' The pagans had their idols. The Philistine army had its holy cow. But, the writer declares, the quality of reassurance that comes from trust in the God who created all things is different entirely.

So what does God protect us from? Obviously he doesn't protect us from misfortune itself. Christians do their share of flooding the bathroom, and losing the front door key, and succumbing to illnesses, and breaking their hearts. We are not people of faith because we want to magic these away. What God *can* protect us from is the harm that these things can do to our inmost beings. And that is made clear in the psalm as well: 'The Lord will keep you from all harm – he will watch over your life.' God can deal completely and thoroughly with the paralysing worry inside us that destroys our courage,

> Let nothing disturb thee, nothing affright thee; All things are passing, God never changeth. Patient endurance attaineth to all things; Whom God possesseth, in nothing is wanting; Alone God sufficeth.
>
> *Teresa of Avila, Spanish nun and writer, 1515–82*

our confidence, and our sense of worth. And because God is addressing the worry inside us, we have the resilience we need to deal with the trouble outside us. With God watching, our true selves, entirely secure in him eternally, can come to no harm.

If you are a Christian, you need not fall apart in a crisis. You know what your first move is going to be.

The reason I belong to the Automobile Association is not that I've got value for money from their breakdown service. In fact, I hardly ever take the car further than Tesco. I get queasy if I push the thing over thirty miles an hour, and I'm not even sure what side of the road they drive on north of the Thames. So I hardly ever call the AA out.

But I am fantastically reassured by the fact that one day, when I've broken down in the pouring rain on a country lane where I can't even see a street light, I will know exactly what the first thing I'm going to do is. I'm not going to despair; I'm going to ring the AA. After that, I'll take things one step at a time.

That is precisely the same reassurance that the writer finds in trusting God in Psalm 121. Where am I going to go first for help? No need to think twice!

Help!
Amen.

The most reassuring truth about God that is revealed in this crisis psalm is that he watches. It's a fabulous image. It's like a mother watching over a child because she promised not to go away until the nightmare has been replaced by sleep. Like someone watching over a friend in a hospital bed, waiting for them to come round after the anaesthetic. Like a sentry wide awake in the long watches of the night, listening for any noise that is the first warning of trouble for his comrades. This is what God is doing . . . always. We cannot be reminded of it too often.

According to the psalm, he watches you as you venture into the places where your feet have a tendency to slip –

great news when you are travelling. He never dozes during his watch – great news during sleepless nights. He keeps an eye on you night and day, whether the sun is a calming pleasure or a blazing hazard. He will watch over your coming and going both now and for evermore – such great news that it should be written next to every Christian's front door as a persistent reminder.

We need to remind ourselves again and again that we are invigilated by a God who has our best interests deep in his heart. If you practise reminding yourself of that during times of stability and happiness, it will come naturally to rely on God to sustain you during times of crisis. An emergency will seem like a challenging time during a happy life, not a moment when you doubt whether you truly have happiness at all.

Keep hold of the reminders in Psalm 121 that God will keep your essential self from harm. It was true 3,000 years ago; it is true today. We no longer live in the days of warriors. But we certainly live in the days of worriers. Where will my help come from? We know! This is a psalm for you and me!

Be happy!
On a postcard, write the last phrase of Psalm 121: 'The Lord will watch over your coming and going both now and for evermore.' Pin it next to your front door, where it will catch your eye as you come and go. When you have learnt it by heart, you can take it down!

Be Happy!
Day 37
Don't give up

Oh dear! I am just about to strip the glitter off another psalm, and I'm sure you are still trying to recover from yesterday's. There is a point to this, though. It turns the psalms from being charming to being useful. It's worth sacrificing some of the syrup that has drenched these ancient hymns if you discover that they contain words that might save your life. Or at least, save your happiness!

> As the deer pants for streams of water,
> so my soul pants for you, O God.
> My soul thirsts for God, for the living God.
> When can I go and meet with God?
> My tears have been my food day and night,
> while people say to me all day long, 'Where is your God?'
> These things I remember as I pour out my soul:
> how I used to go with the multitude,
> leading the procession to the house of God,
> with shouts of joy and thanksgiving among the festive throng.
> Why are you downcast, O my soul?
> Why so disturbed within me?
> Put your hope in God, for I will yet praise him,
> my Saviour and my God.
>
> *Psalm 42.1–6*

Today it is Psalm 42 that could turn into a life-saver. It's the one that has been turned into luscious songs about how a deer pants for water, like our souls long after God, our heart's desire whom we long to worship. Such songs are a delight to sing on occasions when worshipping God is like a long, icy drink on a summer's day – soothing, refreshing, relaxing. And of course, there are occasions when our prayer life is like that.

However, I find myself in an awkward position when I am in church during the stretches when my experience of God is not like that. There aren't many worship songs that begin, 'Lord, I'm honestly not sure whether I want to be here today', or, 'O God, what has happened to the days when our relationship was as fresh as a first date, because now I feel I'm trudging along without you?'

This has not always been the case. Three thousand years ago the hymnbook of the people of God had a much broader range of moods. The psalms risked painful honesty in what they allowed worshippers to say to God. The forty-second one began: 'You've been gone so long, Lord, that when I think of you I feel like a skeletal, emaciated

> My soul is downcast within me;
> therefore I will remember you from the land of the Jordan,
> the heights of Hermon – from Mount Mizar.
> Deep calls to deep in the roar of your waterfalls;
> all your waves and breakers have swept over me.
> By day the Lord directs his love,
> at night his song is with me –
> a prayer to the God of my life ...
> Why are you downcast, O my soul?
> Why so disturbed within me?
> Put your hope in God, for I will yet praise him,
> my Saviour and my God.
>
> *Psalm 42.6–8, 11*

deer, dying of thirst as I scrape my bones along the parched desert dustbowl.' It is a song of despair by a man who can't pray another word.

'My tears have been my food day and night, while people say to me all day long, "Where is your God?"' What made the composer so utterly dejected? He was going through the worst thing a sincere Christian (or a sincere Jew) can experience – a feeling that God has stopped listening, or perhaps never did.

Who was he? Well, he used to be a musician in the temple at Jerusalem. He tells us so: 'I used to go with the multitude, leading the procession to the house of God.' An enemy army from Babylon invaded and captured the Jewish people, and the writer was transported and dragged into exile many miles from home. The suppression he experienced would have been barbaric and physically humiliating, and through it all his conquerors would have taunted and mocked: 'Where is your precious God gone now, when you need him?'

> Pray inwardly, even if you do not enjoy it. It does good, though you feel nothing, see nothing, yea, even though you think you are doing nothing. For when you are dry, empty, sick or weak, at such a time is your prayer most pleasing, though you find little enough to enjoy in it.
>
> *Julian of Norwich, reclusive nun and writer, 1342–1413*

The psalm writer had no answer, because he didn't have the theological understanding of the Holy Spirit that we are fortunate to have. He thought that God lived, actually lived, in the Holy of Holies of the temple at Jerusalem. With the temple in ruins, he thought God was destitute and defeated among the littered bricks. So he literally thought that God was out of earshot, unable to help.

Why can't my faith be like it used to be? We don't need

209

a catastrophic defeat in battle for us to think like that. We just need to be standing in A and E with a sick child, or sitting in a manager's office stunned by the first mention of the word 'redundant', or holding the mobile phone that carries the text: 'I don't love you any more.'

However, there are some wonderfully hopeful trickles of assurance that seep through the psalm and give us suggestions about how to pray when we are so unhappy that we don't see the point. The first is that the composer didn't stop writing, even though he felt that God had stopped listening. He wanted the channels to God to stay open. The irony is that we know something he didn't. God had not been left behind in the rubble that once was the temple. He had gone with the Jews to Babylon. In fact, God had already been at work in Babylon before they even got there. And more than that, he was at work across the entire planet in places that the writer didn't even know existed. Today, when God seems silent, he is nevertheless at work on a staggeringly large scale on planets and suns that are way beyond the range of our telescopes.

> It's tough in the desert. It's bewildering. It's destructive. It's hellish. Yet the testimony of [the Bible] is that out of it comes new growth, new insight, new certainty that a God of love is at home among us.
>
> *Charles Elliot, clergyman and writer, born 1939*

The second feature of the psalm is that the writer was absolutely honest with God. He was not obeying unwritten rules about how he ought to pray. He said it like it was – angry, confused, emotional! And then an extraordinary thing happened. He unexpectedly had a stunning glimpse of God, and it was hugely reassuring. In the barren mountains of Mount Mizar, he had a vision of water cascading all over him: 'Deep calls to deep in the roar of your waterfalls; all your waves and breakers have swept over me.' Unbelievably refreshing if you are a dehydrated deer, and a fantastic reward for being frank with God!

> When prayer is boring, Lord, keep me persistent. When prayer is unanswered, Lord, keep me faithful. And when prayer is impossible, Lord, have mercy.
> Amen.

And third, he went back in his memory to the times when he *did* have assurance that God was with him. He hadn't got his own resources to do it, so he made use of hymns and prayers from a previous generation. Sang them, took courage from them, clung to them! And he wrote about doing so in the psalm: 'At night the Lord's song is with me – a prayer to the God of my life.' I can imagine him lying on the floor in the dark, sleepless with worry, going over the old songs from his temple musician days again and again. And once more there was a dart of hope: 'By day the Lord directs his love at me.' Wonderful! It was gone again as soon as it was there and the psalmist went back to bleakness, but it was undeniable for one deeply comforting moment. When the

Be happy!

Take time to be honest with God. Say what you mean, not what you feel you ought to say. When you have got the things that really matter out in the open, spend the days between now and the end of this forty-day journey anticipating refreshing moments of God's presence, even if they are only fleeting.

writer says, 'Put your hope in God,' it doesn't come easily. It's something said because the old habits are still valuable even when they don't have a shiny feeling of immediate significance.

When you are in a spiritual desert, when you are that

desiccated deer dying for lack of a splash of God, you are not at the end of the story. You are in the middle of the story. You will not always feel like that. The end of the story will be different. The writer, crying out in desperation, was in the middle of his story, not at its conclusion. So how did it end? The Jews *did* go home. The temple *was* rebuilt. And years later, in that very place, the Messiah was born – Jesus the Christ.

Not giving up in prayer! Being honest to God! Looking for refreshment in words that have stood the test of time! 'Put your hope in God, for I will yet praise him.'

Be Happy!

Day 38

Consider your death

'Tell us a tale!' said the children to the storyteller.

'What kind of tale do you want?' asked the old man, as the children settled around his feet.

'A happy tale,' they chorused.

So the storyteller began: 'The grandfather died. The father died. The son died.'

> When the perishable has been clothed with the imperishable, and the mortal with immortality, then the saying that is written will come true: 'Death has been swallowed up in victory.' Where, O death, is your victory? Where, O death, is your sting?
>
> *I Corinthians 15.54–55*

That was the end of the story. The children stared at him, blank and bewildered. It was many years before they understood what the old man had taught them. But when they did understand, it changed the way they lived for the better.

There is a natural order to the way God has organized the world in which we are privileged to live. That order takes us from birth, through vulnerability, into independent life, back to vulnerability, and then to death. And of course, the Christian hope is that death is not the end, but an absorption into eternity in the company of God.

> As Jesus started on his way, a man ran up to him and fell on his knees before him. 'Good teacher,' he asked, 'what must I do to inherit eternal life?' 'Why do you call me good?' Jesus answered. 'No one is good – except God alone. You know the commandments: "Do not murder, do not commit adultery, do not steal, do not give false testimony, do not defraud, honour your father and mother."' 'Teacher,' he declared, 'all these I have kept since I was a boy.' Jesus looked at him and loved him. 'One thing you lack,' he said. 'Go, sell everything you have and give to the poor, and you will have treasure in heaven. Then come, follow me.' At this the man's face fell. He went away sad, because he had great wealth ... The disciples were even more amazed, and said to each other, 'Who then can be saved?' Jesus looked at them and said, 'Humanly, this is impossible, but not with God; all things are possible with God.'
>
> *Mark 10.17–22, 26–27*

It may seem a strange thing to be asked to consider your death while you are reading a book about happiness, but it shouldn't be. The way we live as a society has encouraged us to keep death at arm's length. Some people go through their entire lives without ever seeing a dead body, and that encourages us to attempt to get through life without thinking about a dead body either (except on television, where there is a perplexing fascination for other people's deaths in drama and documentaries).

However, the truth is undeniable. Within more or less seventy years of learning the facts of life, all of us find out, willingly or not, the facts of death.

It is surely an overstatement to suggest that it is possible to have a happy death. But it is certainly possible to have a good death. And the best way to prepare for a good death is to live a good life. Christians who consider their death are able to reach a point of contentment, because they are prepared and can embrace it as part of the way a good God has arranged human destiny.

Sometimes, of course, the natural order is broken, and the results are heartbreaking. It would have been a tragedy if the storyteller's tale had been, 'The grandfather died. The son died. The father died.' But all of us know a family for whom this has been true, and suggesting that we prepare to die well is not meant to diminish in any degree the sadness and confusion of a death that is untimely. If this has been part of your story, I am so sorry. I pray that you will know the exceptional blessing that Jesus promised to those who seek his comfort during their mourning, and that you will never give up on the prospect of being happy in this life and the next.

> It is not darkness that you are going to, for God is light. It is not lonely, for Christ is with you. It is not unknown country, for Christ is already there.
>
> *Charles Kingsley, clergyman and novelist, 1819–75*

There are some practical things that you can do to help you consider your death in a positive way. The first is to put your affairs in order. Write a will, and make sure that those who need the information know where to find it. The rest concern your relationships with people who have been significant during your life. Make peace! Ensure that there is nothing left unsaid, and that there is no unfinished emotional business. Even if there is absolutely no urgency about it, knowing that this has been done will enable you to look at the years ahead with equanimity.

> When it comes to die, make sure all you have to do is die.
>
> *Jim Elliot, martyred missionary to the Auca tribe of Ecuador, 1927–56*

If there is a more pressing reason to anticipate the end of life, talk about death – with those you love and with those who know the medical facts. Be aware of the questions that everyone asks as life comes to a close. Why is this happening now? What has my life been for? Who am I? For some people it is a struggle to put these matters into words, but it can be equally helpful to sit in silence with someone, holding their gaze or their hand. And also, say goodbye! While there is time, say it with its true meaning: 'God be with you.'

There is nothing new about not wanting to engage with the realities of death. People didn't want to do it 2,000 years ago when Jesus walked the earth. A young, wealthy man hunted Jesus out because he didn't want to die. Not one bit! He thought Jesus might be able to help him with this, but he got more than he bargained for.

He was immensely polite to Jesus and, it has to be said, in reply Jesus teased him a bit. He had met people like the rich young man before. And he recognized a genuine desire to be good – perhaps he saw a bit of himself in that. The man set himself the ludicrously unobtainable target of perfection: 'I'll obey every single commandment perfectly and without any failures if the result will be that I can have eternal life.' In reply, Jesus nodded sagely and agreed, 'Yes, that's all you need to do!' I don't know how he kept a straight face!

> Take hold of me,
> Lord Jesus, willing or
> unwilling, rich or poor,
> pious or piteous, and
> don't let go of me until
> I have followed you into
> eternal life.
> Amen.

Then a flood of affection for the guy flowed out of Jesus. But it did not stop him coming out with the most challenging words he ever said to anyone: 'One thing you lack. Go, sell everything you have and give to the poor, and you will have treasure in heaven. Then come, follow me.' Stone me! If he said that to the people he loved, how demanding could he be of the people he didn't take a liking to!

No wonder Jesus' disciples reacted with bewilderment. 'So who on earth can be saved?' they asked. And Jesus' answer was brilliant. For a man or woman to do the impossible and live for ever would take an unprecedented miracle. *The very same kind of miracle that raised Jesus from the dead.*

And that's what it turned out to be all about. This is the way to prepare for a good death. It does not come from denying it, because ultimately you can't. 'Humanly this is impossible, but not with God; all things are possible with God.' When the time comes to die, all you have to do is die. Truly, that's all! God will do absolutely everything else that is required. He will work the miracle.

All you have to do is die. I think I could manage that. Yes! Resurrection – bring it on! Not tonight preferably, if I'm honest. But whenever God is ready. Bring it on!

There's one way I'm different from the rich young man. Rich? OK, there are two ways I'm different from the rich young man. Young? OK, there are three ways I'm different from the . . . oh, I'm getting confused.

What I am trying to say is that, quietly but confidently, I am not walking away from Jesus sad, like the rich young man did. And I'm not afraid, even in these unpredictable days. I'm writing this with a smile the size of the Pacific Ocean. I know where I'm going. Thank you, God!

Be happy!

Plan your funeral. This will be a life-affirming exercise, making you even more appreciative of the people, words and music that God has given to enrich your life so far. It is also a chance to witness to what God has meant to you, and the hope you have about spending eternity with him. Don't use your funeral to settle scores or send hidden messages – sort those things out while you are alive. Instead provide reassurance to those who will eventually attend the event that they are doing something that would give you pleasure.

Be Happy!

Day 39

Declare yourself happy

I went to London's West End to see a new play at Wyndham's Theatre. As I was making my way to seat D16, I saw that someone was already sitting in it. I hate it when that happens! As I began to mumble, 'Excuse me,' I realized who it was – the actor Alan Rickman. Next to him were the actress Frances Barber, and the legendary theatre director Peter Brook and his wife. They checked their tickets and, sure enough, they had D16 to D19.

I began to back out of the row, murmuring, 'I'm sure they will find me somewhere else.' But Alan Rickman was insistent: 'No! We're here as guests of the theatre. If you paid for this seat, you are going to sit in it.' All four of them stood up and moved away. I have no idea where they ended up.

> Be made new in the attitude of your minds; and put on the new self, created to be like God in true righteousness and holiness.
>
> *Ephesians 4.23–24*

I thoroughly enjoyed the play, which I watched with three empty seats beside me. My enjoyment was doubled by the fact that having such a good view had involved budging some of the most famous celebrities alive on the planet.

On the train home I made up my mind to keep the theatre ticket as a souvenir, so I had another look at it. It wasn't D16. It was O16.

If you're happy and you know it clap your hands; If you're happy and you know it clap your hands; If you're happy and you know it and you really want to show it . . .

I told this story to an acquaintance, and she said, 'If only things like that happened to me! I am just not the kind of person to whom lucky things happen.' I've found myself thinking about what she said almost as much as I have thought about the play. I would love to see her liberated from sighing, 'If only things were different, I would be happier.' I believe it is possible that she could accept the unchangeable

> [Moses declared to the people:] 'This day I call heaven and earth as witnesses against you that I have set before you life and death, blessings and curses. Now choose life, so that you and your children may live, and that you may love the Lord your God, listen to his voice, and hold fast to him. For the Lord is your life.'
>
> *Deuteronomy 30.19–20*

things about her, rejoice in what is positive about her, and become a happier person. Those things are choices.

> Most folks are about as happy as they make up their minds to be.
>
> *Abraham Lincoln, sixteenth President of the USA, 1809–65*

If only I hadn't been born so shy! If only I hadn't gone bald! If only my parents had been wealthier! Think again! Your personality, your appearance and your upbringing are not going to change. However, your attitude to them matters much more than the fact of them. No one can ever take your attitude away from you – it is yours to choose.

Writing to Christians who lived in Ephesus, Paul insisted

that it was possible to have a new attitude of mind. In fact, he insisted on it and described it as putting on a new self. And that new self was to be like God – holy and righteous. What an ambition!

Another way in which a new attitude can mirror God's qualities is that the mind of God is constantly focused on solutions. I have no doubt that during the course of my life there have been a million occasions when I have ruined the ideal plan that God had for the world, either by not realizing what would be best or by defying it because I wanted a better personal outcome. However, God seems never to have given up on me. Like a true artist, he never rubs out the blots that have been forced on his drawing. Instead he incorporates them into the picture, constantly recreating his plan with a new solution.

People who are making a success of their lives focus on solutions, not problems. They are honest with themselves, both their strengths and their weaknesses. And they are honest with God, grateful for the potential offered by the strengths and wanting the damage caused by the weaknesses to be forgiven. Then they set about change.

Change! There are no short cuts. If you are to develop new attitudes that remain positive no matter what is happening to you, a change of mind is obligatory. 'Do not conform any longer to the pattern of this world,' wrote Paul in another of the letters that have proved invaluable

We who lived in concentration camps can remember the men who walked through the huts comforting others, giving away their last piece of bread. They may have been few in number, but they offer sufficient proof that everything can be taken from a man but one thing: the last of the human freedoms – to choose one's attitude in any given set of circumstances, to choose one's own way.

Victor Frankl, Austrian psychiatrist and survivor of Auschwitz, 1905–97

to Christians in every subsequent generation, 'but be transformed by the renewing of your mind.'

So how can you renew your mind so that it is not bogged down by feelings that you can't help, but is buoyed up by attitudes over which you have control? I have three suggestions that are positive and life-affirming. I hope they can help you train your mind so that its natural state is to assume happiness.

The first is to coach yourself to have a tolerant mind. This doesn't mean having no convictions of your own; it means having an openness to people with every kind of opinion and lifestyle, listening to them and discerning what is and isn't right to learn from them. At the heart of this is a recognition that every human on our planet, even those with whom you feel you have nothing in common, is regarded by God as precious. He finds them likeable, even if you don't. I have yet to meet a prejudiced person who struck me as happy. Listening to people and trying to discern a way in which your life has improved because your paths have crossed will open your mind. You don't have to agree with them, or copy what they are doing. You don't even have to see them again if you don't want to. But you do have to learn from them. If you simply cannot think of a way in which their actions might make you any happier, try thinking of a way in which *your* actions could make *them* happier. That way the sum total of happiness in the world will have increased, even if it was costly for you.

The second is to develop a resolute mind. The kinds of success that will make you happy come when you have a

> Eternal God, grant me a glimpse beyond the darkness to the morning, a glimpse beyond the cold to the spring, a glimpse beyond the tomb to the resurrection, and let me know what it means to be happy.
> Amen.

definite goal. A goal is different from a dream; it is a dream with a target. And pursuing it requires you to be tenacious. You might have small ambitions or towering ambitions – it genuinely does not matter which is true. Paul wrote to the church in Thessalonica: 'Make it your ambition to lead a quiet life, to mind your own business and to work with your hands.' These are not world-changing goals, but for some people they can give true happiness. In contrast, Paul wrote about himself: 'It has always been my ambition to preach the gospel where Christ was not known.' An immense goal! But I am convinced that Paul, single-minded as he was, died a happy man.

The third is to train yourself to have a youthful mind, regardless of your age. A youthful brain is always open to fresh thoughts and experiences, and not stranded in the potholes of refusal to try something new. Just as physical exercise gives you a young heart, mental exercise gives you a young outlook – and you can't get either slumped in front of the television. New conversations, new friendships and new skills all contribute. So do new foods, new places . . . and not forgetting new plays. Send your mind off on an adventure.

> **Be happy!**
> What has happened during the weeks since you started this spiritual journey that has made you happy? What have you done that has made someone else happy? Have any of your attitudes changed? What would you like God to do for you next?

If you wish, you can declare yourself to be a happy person. It does not mean that there will be no sadness in your life, but it does mean that when events happen that bring sorrow they will not define the way you see yourself. Deep within you, inviolable for all eternity, is the person who God knows and likes, and wants to be glad to be alive. To deny that that person is the real you is deadly. To make a choice that you will let that person shape your attitudes is life-giving.

With only one day left of this spiritual journey, life and death are set before you. Choose life! Choose life! Choose life!

Be Happy!

Day 40

Live!

I have had a long time to think about how this spiritual journey should end. I've been tempted to bring it to a climax with razzamatazz and laughter. That would be the most enjoyable ending, but I don't think it would be the most useful. I would be glad to know that I have written a book that cheers people up, but that would only be part of the objective I had when we set out together forty days ago. I have always hoped that this book will contribute towards a life in which happiness is a steady, underpinning feature of all the months and years that are ahead of you.

A colossal ambition? Yes, you're right! Or it would be, were it not for the fact that Christians live their days knowing that the one they follow and worship has passed through death into resurrection. And that truth, central to the faith of Christians in

> God raised [Jesus] from the dead, freeing him from the agony of death, because it was impossible for death to keep its hold on him. David said about him: 'I saw the Lord always before me. Because he is at my right hand, I will not be shaken. Therefore my heart is glad and my tongue rejoices; my body also will live in hope ... You will fill me with joy in your presence.'
>
> Acts 2.24–26, 28

all times and places, is the reason why this book will not end with raucous rejoicing, but with quiet contentment.

To realize why the resurrection of Jesus is not a matter for fireworks, but for calm happiness, you need to think again about what was happening on the morning that Jesus rose again to life. The women arrived at the tomb with embalming spices – yes. The guards tumbled senseless to the ground – yes. Angels as bright as lightning rolled back the stone – yes. But none of these witnessed Jesus' resurrection. They were witnesses to its aftermath. By the time they got there, they had all missed it. Without help from anyone, Jesus had got on with something that only God could do. Behind the stone, in the deep of night, he had quietly risen from the dead.

> You who dwell in the dust, wake up and shout for joy.
>
> Isaiah 26.19

That is not how Christians celebrate Jesus' resurrection, of course! They celebrate it (depending on their taste) with shouts of alleluia, with sublime choirs and gorgeous colours, with rock bands crescendoing through exultant decibels, with incense and harmony. All these things are life-affirming and marvellous. But they are not in any way like the conditions in which the resurrection of Jesus began. It began with no ceremony whatever, in complete silence, in the cold of a shroud, in the solitude of a tomb.

> Inside the church let happy folk
> The Alleluia chant a hundredfold,
> O Father of thy folk, be thine by right
> The Easter joy, the threshold of the light.
>
> Sedulius Scottus, Irish poet, about 800–60

For those of us who long to have stable happiness in our lives, this is the most important truth about the Christian faith that has ever been revealed.

Unhappiness breaks into your life noisily and chaotically. A trauma strikes without warning, bringing thunderous fear. Disappointments in love cry and throb privately inside you. The death of someone you love deafens you to all other feelings with its anguish and ache. Failed ambitions batter you cruelly and in full view of friends or colleagues. Pain makes your body scream at you.

Only resurrection can permanently overcome unhappiness. But resurrection does not come drawing attention to itself with noise and blaze. It comes silently and subtly, and sometimes it may not even be noticed.

If your life has been blighted by a trauma, resurrection will take place one day when you return to the location where the shock or the violence happened and, for the first time, you are not afraid to be there. In fact, you may not even remember that this was the place, because the memory does not occur to you. That is the quiet happiness of resurrection.

If your emotions have been deeply hurt by love that went wrong or never occurred, resurrection will take place one day when you realize that something delightful has happened to you because of who you are, not because you are one half of a couple. Your sense of the unique goodness that you have added to

> Jesus has turned all our sunsets into dawns.
>
> *Clement of Alexandria, theologian, about 150–215*

the world will gently rise. That is the subtle happiness of resurrection.

If bereavement has brought a wound into your life, resurrection will take place one day when you look at a photograph of the person you miss so intensely, and unexpectedly you find that instead of being pierced by grief you are smiling at a memory. That is the tender happiness of resurrection.

If the ambitions that drove you have come to nothing,

resurrection will take place one day when you experience something new and realize that your life has value not because of what you achieve, earn or own, but because of the person you are. That is the calm happiness of resurrection.

And finally one day, when the pain that takes your joy away can get no worse, resurrection will take place when you shrug off the body that has burdened you and step effortlessly forward to where God is waiting.

> Lord God of joyful life,
> open wide your arms
> – I'm on my way!
> Amen.

When unhappiness weighs most onerously upon you, those are the circumstances most similar to the setting in which the resurrection first took place. It may be that your happiness has already returned in the dark and dust, and all that is needed now in order for you to realize it is for the stone to roll away. Every vivid atom of God's good creation is crying out to you: 'Live!'

I believe that a time will come when happiness will be complete and boundless. The Christian hope is that Jesus the Risen One has pushed back the boulder that separated God from his creation and made it possible for humankind to take the journey that he has already taken, from life through death into life. We will stand alongside Jesus the Saviour in the presence of the loving and welcoming God. An eternity of happiness will lie uncharted before us, ready for us to explore.

The closing words of the Bible invite us to anticipate that peace will be made an unending state, for 'there will be no more death or mourning'. They lead us to expect that justice will be restored permanently for those who have suffered oppression in the world, with the end of 'crying and pain, for the old order of things has passed away'. And they assure us that God will bring about the end of unhappiness once and for all, because 'he will wipe every tear from their eyes'. Imagine how that will be greeted by the residents of countries we have visited over the past forty days – Sri Lanka, Angola, the Dominican Republic. Imagine what it will mean for those you know who have carried heavy burdens through the earthly part of their lives. And for you!

When that moment comes, we will look back on the happy moments that have illuminated our lives and smile. They were wonderful, but they merely gave us a taste for the perfect happiness that God has always had in store as the destiny of the creation he loves. They made us glad to be alive, but they only illuminated palely the reality of what it means to be raised from the dead.

I have no idea at all what to expect at that moment. It is quite possible, of course, that it will be accompanied by trumpets, fireworks and triumph. That would indeed be spectacular. However, it would suit me well to enter God's presence in a completely different fashion. I would be very happy indeed to approach the God whose love has moulded and enriched my life in the manner of Jesus' resurrection – quiet, inconspicuous and with a humble content that all the purposes of life have been fulfilled. And as I take those happy steps I will be whispering in breathless wonder, 'Glory, glory, glory, glory!'

> **Be happy!**
> Write about happiness on your blog, and on Facebook and Twitter. Do all you can, whenever you can, to make your friends happy. Tell people what impact reading this book has had on you. Write to me at be.happy.40.days@ googlemail.com to let me know what you are discovering about happiness. Live!